SPEED WRITE
YOUR LIFE STORY

Also by Mark Victor Hansen

BOOKS

Chicken Soup for the Soul series—
  254 different books in print
The One Minute Millionaire
Cracking the Millionaire Code
Cash in a Flash
*How to Make the Rest of Your Life
  the Best of Your Life*
The Aladdin Factor
Dare to Win
The Richest Kids in America
The Miracle of Tithing
The Power of Focus
The Miracles in You
Out of the Blue

Master Motivator
You Are the Solution
You Have a Book in You
Speed Write Your First Book
*Speed Write Your Personal Life Story
  (Your Autobiography)*
Speed Edit Your First Book
Speed Write Your Amazing Publishing Plan
Speed Write Your First Screenplay
Speed Write Your Irresistible Title and Subtitle
Speed Write (and Deliver) Your Killer Speech
Visualizing Is Realizing
Dreams Don't Have Deadlines
Ask!

AUDIOS

*How to Think Bigger than You
  Ever Thought You Could Think*
Dreams Don't Have Deadlines
Visualizing Is Realizing

Sell Yourself Rich
Chicken Soup for the Soul series
The One Minute Millionaire
Cracking the Millionaire Code

Also by Steve Gottry

BOOKS

The On-Time, On-Target Manager
  (Coauthored with Ken Blanchard)
Common Sense Business
A Kick in the Career (Coauthored with
  Linda Jensvold Bauer)
The Screenwriters Story-Planning Guide
Options (Karla Gottry, as told to Steve
  Gottry)

BOOKS IN THIS SERIES WITH MARK VICTOR HANSEN:

Speed Write Your First Book
*Speed Write Your Personal Life Story
  (Your Autobiography)*
Speed Edit Your First Book
Speed Write Your Amazing Publishing Plan
Speed Write Your First Screenplay
Speed Write Your Irresistible Title and Subtitle
Speed Write (and Deliver) Your Killer Speech

AUDIOS AND VIDEOS

The Story of Jesus for Children (Screenplay;
  currently in 176 languages)
Jacob's Gift (Screenplay; adaptation based
  on the bestseller by Max Lucado)

Wondrous Myths and Legends (Sony
  Wonder animated series, with David
  Anderson)
The On-Time, On-Target Manager CD
  (Coauthored with Ken Blanchard)

SPEED WRITE YOUR LIFE STORY

(Your Autobiography)

From Blank Spaces to Great Pages in Just 90 Days

MARK VICTOR HANSEN
AND STEVE GOTTRY

MEDIA

Published 2021 by Gildan Media LLC
aka G&D Media
www.GandDmedia.com

Front Cover design by David Rheinhardt of Pyrographx

Interior design by Meghan Day Healey of Story Horse, LLC

Library of Congress Cataloging-in-Publication Data is available upon request

ISBN: 978-1-7225-0327-7

10 9 8 7 6 5 4 3 2 1

When you fill in the blanks . . .

*. . . you fill in the empty spaces and places
in the lives of your readers.*

Where there is numbing sameness,
you bring abundant variety.

Where adventure is missing,
you create exciting journeys in the mind.

Where there is despair,
you offer meaningful hope.

Where faith is lacking,
you offer a reason to believe.

Where love has not found a home,
you open the doors of the heart.

When someone needs a friend,
you become a soul mate.

Yes, *your* words have AMAZING POWER!

Bring Your Story to Life

You're reading this book because you have a story to tell!

It's been a dream of yours to write it—possibly for years! Or perhaps only months, weeks, or days. Maybe the idea occurred to you just yesterday or today, when this book came to your attention.

The story that is still captive inside you is YOUR PERSONAL LIFE STORY!

The nature or focus of your specific story doesn't matter. What DOES matter is that you write it. And, WE'RE HERE TO HELP!

We are going to empower you to write the story of your life in NINETY DAYS or fewer, investing only TWENTY-TWO MINUTES of time per day!

You say you don't believe us?

Well, we both know it can be done. We've done it!

The length of your first effort is not what's important. The outcome is the product of your decision, desire, dedication, and determination to write, write, and write some more. In the end, you will be proud of what you have accomplished! People in your life will want to read it, and they will enjoy it!

What happens after that is entirely up to you. Will you enjoy the process of writing to the extent that you will want to work on additional projects in our series? Will you want to find a publisher for your future work? Do you want to self-publish your book or offer it as an online download—either free or for sale? Do you want to find a literary agent and launch a new career as an author? Only **YOU** can determine the answers to those questions. Our role is simply to help you right now, then, later on, give you worthwhile information about your options. (But that's in other SPEED WRITE books.)

Whatever you decide, we will stand behind you! There are other books in "Mark and Steve's Writers Wisdom Series"—now or in the future—that will guide you through the myriad aspects of selling, marketing, and even (gulp!) speaking in public about your book.

We know that you have a story ready to burst out of you, and it's time to share with it the world! By following the plan in this book, you can achieve your goal quicker than you think! So, start today, and fill in the blanks.

For additional series information and product support, please go to www.SpeedWritingBooks.com.

Web Site: www.SpeedWritingBooks.com

Please send your comments and suggestions to Steve at gottry@ mac.com. He will do his best to respond to you on behalf of himself and Mark.

—Mark and Steve

Introduction

You have something no one else in the entire world has. Your story! Your memories! They are unique in every way . . . from your birth until today.

The uniqueness of your life story makes it important that you share it with those you love today, as well as with future generations. The reason it's important is because they have so much to learn from you. Your life-time of acquired wisdom is truly worth a fortune.

Have you ever wished that you had asked more questions of those ancestors you were fortunate enough to meet? Your great great-grandparents, possibly your grandparents, maybe even your own parents? Aunts and uncles? Departed cousins?

Well, that's what this book is all about. We wrote it to provide a loosely-structured way to recall all your memories—the events and people in your life who contributed to the person you are today. We are going to be asking you lots of questions, and you will see that we provided open space for you to write down your answers.

But, please don't be intimidated. It really isn't necessary for you to answer every one of them. Because we don't know you personally, we are simply posing general questions. Later on, you will use your answers to write an actual book that you can have printed in any quantity you choose. Those books will make wonderful gifts to parents, children, grandchildren—in fact, every member of your family, and possibly close friends, too. And, as you know, some "memoirs" actually become huge bestsellers. (And, you don't need to be "famous" to be in this league. You just need to think back on your life and remember and write about the most significant things you can. Those things that could change lives!)

Another important consideration: it may be more effective for you to depart from pure "Linear Structure." By that, we mean you really don't have to begin with "I was born in (city) on (birthdate). You can begin with an interesting, engaging event or thought. We believe the most important purpose of your finished book is to impart the wisdom you have acquired over the years. In other words, you are sharing lessons for life, and telling stories about challenges and heartbreaks, as well as the "fun times."

It is often effective to begin with an *experience* that your reader may not know about. For example, Mark might share something like this:

"I am proof that *persistence* can pay big dividends. Years ago, Jack Canfield and I called on countless publishers in an effort to sell our first *Chicken Soup for the Soul* book. We could have easily gotten discouraged after being rejected by the first (twenty?) publishers we called on. But we stuck with it. Instead of giving up, our series of impactful books became international best sellers, with more than (500,000,000?) books sold around the world. Winston Churchill famously said, 'Success consists of going from failure to failure without loss of enthusiasm.'"

Steve might tell about how he learned about *"boldly asking* for what you want."

"In 1965, I learned that The Beatles were scheduled to perform a live concert in Bloomington, Minnesota. So, I contacted the concert promoter and told him, 'I am a photographer and writer for *TWIN CITIES A'GO GO.* (A small publication covering the music scene.) Is there going to be a news conference?' Of course, there was one scheduled, and the promoter mailed a press pass and concert tickets to me. I was able to talk to all four Beatles and take their pictures from a distance of four feet . . . using a $25 Minolta 35 mm camera I bought while a junior in high school. I still have the press pass, the camera, and the original negatives—and the pictures are framed and hanging on the walls in my home office." (Steve is assuming that many people still know who The Beatles were!)

Just think for a moment! You have your own lesson or "hook" with which you can begin your personal life story. It could be something like, "The day I first met my spouse, I knew for certain that he/she was "The One." So, I established a plan to win his/her heart. The first thing I did was. . . ." (Then simply tell the story!)

The important thing is that you BEGIN. The old saying, "a journey of a thousand miles begins with one step" certainly applies to writing ANY book, any screenplay, any stage play, or even any marketing or publishing plan.

First Things First

Gather Your Tools and Resources

We want to do everything we possibly can to make this significant project easy, engaging, and enjoyable. After all, we both love writing, and have written tons of books, videos, movies, plays . . . and on and on. In the process, we have discovered the "keys to ease"; little secrets that help uncomplicate writing for everyone.

An extremely helpful **first step** is to gather your tools and resources.

Because this book is about your personal life story, you will be basing it on your memories. And where do you store your memories? Here are some obvious possibilities:

☐ Photo albums, videos, home movies, slides . . .

☐ Your "Memory Box." This may contain old report cards, newspaper clippings, diplomas, awards, Military Discharge papers, birth certificates . . .

☐ Your Journals or diaries: if you have recorded memories of your life in writing, this could be a fun time to do a full review!

The **second step** is to gather what you need to keep track of your thoughts and ideas. (This applies to writing your personal life story, as well as any future writing projects you choose to pursue.)

☐ Keep a note pad, note book, and pen and pencil, near you at all times, so that you can jot down your ideas as they come to your mind.

☐ As an alternative, you can take your notes on the "Notes" app that can be loaded onto (or comes with) most smart phones. (Or you can send text messages/emails to yourself that contain your ideas.)

☐ Some of us still reply on voice recorders . . . either the record app on smart phones, or even a separate tiny digital recorder. (They are often $40 or less, and can record several hours of your ideas on them. There are some recorders than can even transcribe your spoken word into text in the word processing program on your laptop computer.

☐ Speaking of transcriptions, there are a number of websites to which you can upload your recordings for inexpensive transcriptions that can be copied and pasted directly into your working manuscript. Mark personally uses and recommends NONOTES .COM, IDICTATE.COM, or ORGANIZATIONX.COM. Of course, if you are using an offshore transcription service, the spelling and grammar may not be perfect, so you will have to proofread carefully.

You're Ready to Write!

This is the big moment! You're ready to start writing! No excuses. No delays. You need to start now!

Track Your Time

We believe that you can write your life story in 90 days by investing just 22 minutes each day. That's why we're asking you to track your time on the charts we've included (see following pages).

Don't punish yourself if you write for *more* than 22 minutes. Don't punish yourself if you write for *fewer* than 22 minutes. We're not here to make you feel guilty. We want you to enjoy this! The purpose of life, we feel, is the joy of creation. We enjoyed creating this book for you. We want you to thrill to the process the way we do.

How Is It Going?

Even if you've only written 22 minutes a day for 12 days, we really don't mind. That's because you'll be able to apply new ideas as you write. Nothing wrong with that! Just remember to write every day . . . and record your dates and numbers of minutes. If you fall short a few minutes, just add it on when you have sufficient time to catch up and especially when you are on-fire with inspiration.

The First 30 Days

DATE	TIME	WHAT I DID

Days 31 to 60

DATE	TIME	WHAT I DID

Days 61 to 90

DATE	TIME	WHAT I DID

Structuring Your Manuscript: The Parts of Your Story

Here is a list of possible topics and sections that you may want to consider for inclusion in your life story: (yes, this is basically linear.)

1. Your birth, date, day, time, where born. (Any unusual events/ circumstances.)
2. Your family heritage. Immigrants, any travels back to the countries of your origin?
3. Best memories of your parents and grandparents.
4. Siblings.
5. Grade school memories, best friends, favorite teachers, activities.
6. Most important lessons learned.
7. Saddest memories (Illnesses, broken bones.)
8. Junior high years: (Favorite Subjects, Best Friends, Activities.)
9. Learning to drive. First Car? (Any tickets/Accidents?)
10. First date(s).
11. High school: Activities, Awards, Best Friends, Newly Acquired Interests/Hobbies. Jobs? (Did you have to drop out of school to help your family financially?)
12. Prom?

13. Did you attend college/graduate? Major/minor? Why did you choose a specific college? Activities/sports? Friends/relationships?
14. Graduate School/Advanced Degrees?
15. Military Service? Branch? Rank? Special Training? Travel? (Where?) Were you involved in any conflicts? Do you make any special (life-long) bonds? Injuries?
16. Career Path, Favorite Jobs, and Why?
17. Chosen Activities as an adult? Hobbies?
18. Religion/Politics/Service Clubs/Toastmasters? (Try not to start any fights!)
19. Personal Favorites? Food/Movies/Music/Books?

Flashbacks and fast-forwards

As we have already suggested, your personal life story might best be told in NON-LINEAR style. (NOT, "I was born in (city) in (year)." Begin with an engaging story or thought. ("Chase Scene" first, then another chase scene at the end.)

Movies and books that include meaningful, purposeful flashbacks and fast-forwards are often more captivating that the 1-2-3 or A-B-C approach. "Surprise" is one of the most effective tools you can use to keep your readers engaged.

YOU are the Star!

YOU are the *protagonist* (hero) of your personal life story. One of the things that makes movies, novels, biographies, and your story interesting are the challenges you (and other characters) have faced. This can take the form of one or more *antagonists*. (Also known as your *nemesis*.) One of the best known and obvious examples is the antagonist/nemesis faced by Luke Skywalker, Princess Leia, and Han Solo in the *STAR WARS* films—in the form of the quite unpleasant Darth Vader.

But your nemesis does not need to be an actual adult person to provide a challenge. Your adversary could be an animal, an inanimate object (a car), weather challenges, as well as a coworker, or dare we mention it . . . even your children.

1. For many decades, a nemesis has often turned out to be an unprovoked "bully." (This is HUGE area of concern these days. But it really is a timeless issue.)

   a. Explain when you were bullied.

   _____

   _____

   _____

   b. How severe was the bullying?

   _____

   _____

   _____

   c. Were you hurt emotionally/physically?

   _____

   _____

   _____

   d. Did you bully back? (Get even?)

   _____

   _____

   _____

   e. What did you learn from the experience?

   _____

   _____

   _____

f. What would you recommend to anyone who is bullied?

_____

_____

_____

g. What about rejection? Shunning? Being ignored? Is that the same thing?

_____

_____

_____

2. Suggestions about your nemesis:
   a. Is there/was there someone in your life who wanted the same things you want? That person is often your "adversary" or "competitor."

   _____

   _____

   _____

   b. Do you feel/have you felt that you still have "active competitors?"

   _____

   _____

   _____

   c. What are your thoughts on "evil in the world?" Do you believe that "good" will ultimately, eventually "win?"

   _____

   _____

   _____

SPECIFIC QUESTIONS TO CONSIDER

Many of the questions that follow are presented in linear order . . . in the same order in which people live their lives. Other questions are based on "stream of consciousness." They tend to interrupt the logical flow and head down a different path.

1. Who have been the positive influences in your life? (Teachers, parents, siblings, friends, etc.)
   a. What **teacher** (if any?) made a significant difference in your life? How?

   _____

   _____

   _____

Both Mark and Steve have enjoyed memorable experiences with teachers who made a real difference. Here is Mark's reflection:

"I was born into a loving Danish immigrant family. We lived in Little Denmark—Waukegan, Illinois. We went to the Danish Brotherhood every Saturday night and the Danish Lutheran Church every Sunday. I thought everyone in the world naturally spoke Danish. We had few books in our home. (Nearly none.) As a result, I had reading difficulties early on. I was in remedial reading from first and second grade with a sweetheart of a mature woman, who was bigger than life!

"Later on, John Reinhardt would inspire me to love reading. I would ultimately take it on as a positive and life changing addiction, and eventually become the world's bestselling author. (He would never have guessed that!) Mr. Reinhardt was the great and inspiring teacher who made literature come alive and vibrantly live in our minds, hearts, souls, and experiences. He was much like the man Robin Williams played in the *Dead Poet's Society*, he was eclectically insightful, a polymath, thespian, and could see more in his students than they could see in themselves. His class was challengingly compelling. He expected us to own our assignments and see their comparison to the events happening and related nightly on Walter Cronkite and the news. He wanted each of us to live up to our fullest potential—now and forever.

"He knew us by name and called us out on our lives. He cared deeply and expected us to respect the wonders of reading widely, deeply, and coming around to contribute greatly to the world. He was the most sophisticated and comprehensively informed human I had experienced up to that time. Like most of us in the class, he made a difference that made a difference. I would rank his teaching the Socratic Method to be similar to Aristotle teaching Alexander the Great, which he taught us inclusive of Greek Mythology and how it would impact the rest of our lives.

"My parents had passed away by the time I won the *Book of the Year Award* to be presented at the American Bookseller's Annual convention, in front of thousands of people at McCormick Place in Chicago, Illinois. In lieu of my beloved parents, I invited Mr. and Mrs. Reinhardt to attend. I told the audience that 'reading gives us freedom. Reading gives us the ability to think deeply and serve greatly. Reading invites us to simulate experiences and holographically image them in our minds-eye. Reading inspires us absorb the wisdom and insights of thousands of years of thinking, experience, and results. I had come from a loving Danish immigrant family but we had no books in our home. I did little reading until my great and inspiring English teacher encouraged, excited and, demonstrated to me the wonderful world of reading. As a result, I became a lifelong learner.'

Mark with John Reinhardt and his wife.

"'My sophomore English teacher is here in the room as my guest today, and I humbly ask him to stand and ask you to applaud the front-end reason of why I wanted to become—and became—an author. Please recognize Mr. John Reinhardt and his wife from Waukegan, Illinois, my home town.'

"They cried in response to me honoring them. I was crying, too.

"I was in John Reinhardt's English Class when it was announced President John F. Kennedy had just been shot and killed in Dallas. Each of us became a bucket of tears, because Reinhardt had us read *Camelot* and see the movie, which was just released. JFK's favorite movie was Camelot and he was idealistically rebuilding America along the lines of King Arthur's example.

"Reinhardt said, 'The high school principal has announced that school is over for today in deference and respect to our grieving for our esteemed and revered President JFK.' Reinhardt added, 'Call your parents, get permission, and those who want to stay and discuss President Kennedy and what it means to us can stay. We will talk.' Almost everyone made a call and stayed. We talked from 2:00 P.M. until 5:00 P.M. It was riveting and unforgettable. The memories are still profoundly imprinted in my mind. I became a Kennedy scholar and own almost every book written about JFK because of that extraordinary experience."

_____

Steve's example is his late and beloved Seventh grade English teacher, Ole Loing, for whom he was honored to write a eulogy.

Steve was a Seventh Grade student at the Mountain Lake (Minnesota) Public School when he became ill with rheumatic fever. He was confined to bed for almost ten months, and was forced to drop out of school. (Remember, at that time, there was no Internet and no "distance learning." So, Steve had to repeat seventh grade. In looking back, that was a blessing.

You see, in his first "go" at Junior High, Steve got an "F" at the end of his first quarter of English. It was his first failing grade in school, and he was devastated! (At the time, he thought that his English teacher, "Miss Kay-Something-or-other," was an "ugly Battle-Axe." Back then, that was a common term for teachers whom students didn't much appreciate.

When Steve returned to Seventh Grade the following fall, he was pleased to learn that Miss Battle-Axe had moved on. (He had hoped that her final destination was some Federal Prison!)

That's when Steve met his new English teacher, Mr. Ole Loing . . . a pleasant surprise if there ever was one! Mr. Loing was a young, bright, recent-college-graduate Scandinavian. With not one drop of "Battle-Axe" blood in his body!

Mr. Loing had no idea that Steve had flunked English the previous year. But he wisely somehow sensed that Steve had ADHD, something that wasn't even suspected as an issue at that time. So, he worked with Steve to structure "special assignments" that were a match to Steve's interests and abilities. And it worked! Steve got "A" grades throughout Seventh Grade, "fell in love" with

Steve with Ole at coffee just before he died. (Photo taken in Princeton, MN, by Steve's eldest daughter, Michelle, who is now an Encouraging Third-Grade teacher herself).

English and writing, took Advanced Composition from Ms. Dorothy Tweet (her real name!) in High School, pursued a University of Minnesota degree in Journalism, and has earned his living as a writer ever since graduation. (Yes, Ole Loing was WAY ahead of his time! Steve credits Ole as his "life-changing Encourager!")

Ole was a Liberal Democrat; Steve was a Conservative Republican. But they respected each other. They had a bond that ignored mostly meaningless differences.

b. **Parents**: Were you raised by two parents at home? If not, why not? What lessons did you learn from your dad? What lessons from your mom?

_____

_____

_____

c. **Grandparents**: Did you know them? Were they alive when you grew up?

_____

_____

_____

d. **Siblings**: Do you have siblings? What have you learned from them?

_____

_____

_____

MORE QUESTIONS ABOUT YOUR SIBLINGS:

1. How many sisters and brothers did you have? What do you remember of them and your experiences both good and bad?

_____

_____

_____

2. How did you parents treat each of them and you? What is your most memorable feeling?

_____

_____

_____

3. Did you feel better or worse with the addition of a baby sister or brother?

_____

_____

_____

4. Whom of your siblings were you closest to? Why?

_____

_____

_____

5. Did any sibling offend you, your values, or your future?

_____

_____

_____

6. Did you feel too much or too little responsibility? More or less than your siblings or friends?

_____

_____

_____

7. Were your parents respected, appreciated and loved?

_____

_____

_____

Here are Mark's and Steve's candid "Sibling Thoughts." (Presented as an example.)

First, Mark:

I am cheerfully from a family of three siblings, all boys. We were all enthusiastic workers because our dad made sure we didn't take anything for granted. We had to figure out our own way to earn spending money which resulted in lawn mowing, window washing, snow shoveling, and greeting card sales. I used to over-hear my mother tell the patrons at Dad's bakery, as well as Mabel at the grocery store, "*I have the best boys on the block.*" That's a lot to live up to. I can proudly say that we all did our best to live up to her claim. My brothers and I went on to have lucrative businesses through which we were each successful in our own right. Mom's nightly prayers with each of us from birth ended with the line, "and may Bay, Eric, Mark, and Brian be happy and healthy." Each of my brothers mastered and satisfied their life's destiny.

My younger brother Brian is, as my mother loved to say, "two years and three days younger." Our proximity in age had great benefits for me. When we were little, we did everything together. We played, worked, lived, and moved in unison. I got to learn and practice my leadership, promotion, and sales skills on him. He was such a willing student.

We got in trouble together, most often provoked and instigated by me. In her attempt to master and keep running a home filled with the testosterone of four hyper active sons and our Dad, she was the one who had to spank us. It was rare but occasional. We deserved it, I am sure. She never hurt us, but wanted to make us aware of our digression from her rules—like the simplicity of safely crossing a street by looking first to the left and then to the right. She repeatedly told us to mind her or suffer the consequences—i.e. a spanking or time out.

One vivid memory comes from my early desire to see the world, travel extensively, and experience it first-hand. This is a lust that has never wavered. We were strictly told to stay in our ultra-safe neighborhood where we knew all our friendly neighbors by sight. I was five years old, maybe almost six, when I grabbed the hand of my little brother—who was 3 or 4 years old—and off we went to explore the world as we knew it.

It was in the summer when we had most of the day to play and explore. Our father worked a lot and our mother worked part time, as I recall. Being the older and wiser brother, I suggested we walk downtown to dad's bakery. We had done the trip many—even hundreds—of times in the back seat of our parents' maroon 1952 Dodge station wagon.

The directions were easy. Head east half mile on Glen Flora until it dead-ended by the hospital, then go south 2 miles on Sheridan until we got downtown. Two-and-a-half miles was a long walk for 4 and 6-year-old boys—especially with so many things to see along the way. We had sidewalks all the way, but needed to cross several busy intersections.

Upon arrival at our parent's bakery, we were shocked that our father was not happy with our adventurous achievement. After we got a stern talking-to, we were escorted to the back seat of the Dodge station wagon and were returned home, where we were confined for several days until we learned not to venture out beyond a 2-block radius.

My mother's frequently repeated viewpoint was: "I have things to do, places to go, people to meet." While we were missing, our mother was panicked, curious then furious, and then white hot mad. She looked everywhere she thought we could be. She loudly

SHOUTED our names, to no avail. She called all of the neighbors, assuming we had gone into someone's home without notifying her. There was no response and no answer to where we were.

She feared we had been kidnapped, though she couldn't figure out who'd want us. After an hour of sheer fear, my Dad called her and told her, "The boys are here. Yes, I mean at the bakery. I don't know how they did it. Marky said he walked them here." (Inwardly, I believe dad, a man who loved to explore, travel, go on adventures, and visit foreign lands secretly was proud that we did it, though he could not tell my mother, who was rightfully furious.)

When we got home, mom spanked us with the duffer . . . her slipper . . . and put us in separate corners of our dining room. We proceeded, as if on cue, to cry. When mom walked out of the room, we couldn't stop laughing—deep profound belly laughs. We had explored the world and returned safely—our first stellar self-generated achievement—without horribly serious repercussions. Mom moved through our home with speed, grace, and agility. She wore flat slippers that she called duffers. They loudly slapped the back of her heels when she walked, so we knew her whereabouts. We heard her coming.

When mom re-entered the room, we immediately turned on the tears. After a bucket of tears, she couldn't help herself, she was so relieved that her darling prodigal sons had returned from the far country safe that, having a hard time holding back a smile, she said "Okay then, have you learned your lesson to obey me?" In unison, we responded "yes."

"You are released again, but STAY NEAR HOME IN THE NEIGHBORHOOD AND COME WHEN I CALL YOU TO DINNER. DO YOU BOTH HEAR ME?"

"Yes, Mommy," we replied.

*   *   *

My brother, Eric, is four years older than I am. Eric tested the limits of our parents the most. Mom often said he had a hot temper. Eric made life unusual and exciting sometimes. I remember one time, Dad brought us up to the Wisconsin/Illinois State Line where it was legal to buy fireworks. Eric, Brian, and I had our own money to buy basically whatever we wanted: sparklers, exploding caps, fire crackers, pyrotechnics—class B special fireworks from China. We each loaded up on them.

Eric was particularly fond of cherry bombs. At night, he liked to invite his friends over and give them explosive pyrotechnical shows. Mom had just received an extraordinarily detailed and totally cherished birdbath from Dad for her last birthday. She loved watching all the birds come into our back yard and dance around, play, preen, and clean themselves in her four-inch deep birdbath.

Eric wondered whether or not cherry bombs would explode under water, so he couldn't resist the challenge of testing them with an audience of his best buddies, Brian, and me at dusk on July Third. He lit the fuse, threw the cherry bomb into the birdbath, and "viola!" it exploded perfectly under water, as if on command. It completely demolished the birdbath, blasting it into thousands of pieces.

It felt like it was time to "head for the hills," as the cliché says. Except there were no hills and the screams from us onlookers brought both Mom and Dad running out of our home thinking someone was hurt. The bird bath lay in ruins. Our parents were temporarily speechless and then we heard them exclaim, "Eric, get in the house this minute and don't come out until we say so. The party is over—everyone go home now!" And that permanently ended our childhood trips to the State Line to buy Fourth of July fireworks.

One more memory of my brother, Eric. When he went to the dentist as a child, he bit the dentist out of pain and anger. When I went to the same dentist, the first thing Dr. "Whatever" said was, "If you don't bite me, I'll give you a quarter." Eric had made him fear the wrath of the Hansen boys. I, of course, took the quarter and never bit the dentist.

As the reigning family patriarch, Eric now coordinates our annual family trips and cruises for all three families. Meaning that he has successfully put together annual events with the Hansens and the Petersens on my mother's side of the family and the Waldens on my mother's sister's side of the family. We all grew up together. We all shared some Christmas and Thanksgiving Holidays together. We all more or less knew one another, are about the same age, and have played, worked, and gone to school together. Fortunately, we all get along brilliantly well. So, Eric contacts as all and tells us what potential annual vacations we can vote on and then take together. It's amazing how many in our extended family repetitively and happily show up on these adventurous journeys.

We have joyfully cruised through the Mexican Caribbean with everyone regaling one another with delightful and forgotten stories of our family's experiences—its joys, triumphs, delights, and failures. These are unforgettable trips and create memories of how much our family loves and is thankful for one another. Eric and his wife Lois, along with our cousin Jimmy Petersen, have chronicled our family ancestry charts, which are amazingly detailed and complete, looking back more than a hundred years. On our trips together, these are shown, shared, and explained. What's amazing is that they have stimulated family members to go back to what was affectionately called "The Old Country,"

Denmark, and visit where we all originated. While there last, Eric and Jimmy discovered even more relishable and tellable stories of our ancestry.

Below I share the words that I wrote for my recently departed brother Bay's memorial service. Note that, for me, the hardest eulogy to deliver is for a relative. The emotional memories are deep and resonant. As I tried to share such things—especially when surrounded by more relatives and lifelong friends—it choked me up and was beyond difficult.

*   *   *

Bay's Memorial:
by Mark Victor Hansen

Ralph Waldo Emerson said, "The greatest gift you can ever give is your presence." So, our entire family thanks each and every one of you for coming to honor the memory of my big brother, Bailey Dewayne Hansen.

We can only stop time in four ways: with photos, memories, feelings, and a funeral.

1. Photos can be either still and motion photography, as we have seen from Kris Lee Hansen and later from Cousin Earl Petersen.

2. Stories—that we tell and will re-tell and will remember triggered by others here today and tonight.

And 3. Our memories . . . today, everyone has delighted in the memory or the memorialization of my beloved big brother.

4. Feelings tend to gush and rush us—often to tears—at a funeral or a memorial. Sharing these memories of family, friends, work, education, and a life well lived revitalize a man's life memory. They show that Bay's life was joyously fulfilling and thrilling to him.

His memory and his life were so precious in so many special ways. For me, Bay was a mentor in many ways. I looked up to Bay. He was my earliest and easiest up-close-and-personal role model. Being 11 years older than I am, he was good looking—even handsome, suave, occasionally elegant. I watched the tantalizingly excitement of him going to two proms his junior and senior high school years, dressed to the nines in a tuxedo; poised, calm, and he had the strong demeanor, the then famous actor Clint Eastwood. He was cool, the strong silent type who just confidently knew that he knew. He had a photographic memory, great art painting and sculpting abilities, brand new blue on white Chevy Bel Air car, a hog Harley Motorcycle, a lovely girlfriend, a high paying job with money in his pocket and lots of friends who loved him and hung out with him at our home.

Bay was brilliant at the oily secrets of machinery, mechanics, electronics, and he could fix anything. The top of his hands had almost perpetual scratch marks on them from working on the innards of car engines. To this day, when I scratch myself and draw blood, I can see in my minds eye Bay doing the same, licking his wound, not allowing himself to feel the pain, and proceeding to finish fixing the car engine like nothing happened. Bay was quietly effective, strong, and stoic to the max. I was not. I tried to do what he did, but I have almost zero mechanical aptitude. I was destined to be a white glove guy.

As a car aficionado, Bay was a member of "Gear Jammers Car Club" and had a little hanging metal plaque announcing the same in 1957. It was on the bumper of his car. So, when he "dragged the loop" (i.e. cruised downtown Waukegan, Illinois) people could clearly see he was part of the "in-crowd." I was then only nine years old. Bay would kindly allow me be with him and sometimes hang with his buddies. I could pretend I was a big, cool guy.

Basking in their respective togetherness and coolness on a Friday night when they all came over to our home and hang out raised my young self-esteem, before I knew or understood what that even meant.

As a car-nut, Bay essentially bought a new GM car every year. He let my younger brother, Brian, and me help him wax it when we were nine and seven years old, respectively. Then, he would take us to "scoop the loop" in downtown Waukegan.

Bay was athletically strong, fit, and a body-builder. He got me interested in fitness, body building, and health. He was also a hunter with both a gun and bow and arrow. Bay taught me the skills with a bow and arrow. He took me to the bow and arrow range and I actually got good at target practice. We went carp fishing together. Fishing in a fast-moving river is interesting because, unless the fish are near the surface, the gushing water distorts the image of exactly where they are. I broke many arrows learning that lesson. To bring home fish for mom to cook was exciting for me as a kid, supported by my big brother who taught me how to do it. Mom said: "Why don't you boys shoot real tasty fish?" Bay would smile and say "We can only shoot what's in the Des Plaines River, Mom. Carp is it."

As a nine-year old, I started delivering the Tribune and Sun Times as a paperboy. It was frequently freezingly below zero, sometimes as low as twenty below zero. Without asking for Bay's help, he saw my flimsy gloves were insufficient to keep my hands warm, so he volunteered and gave me a giant pair of expensive mittens—deep weather mittens he had gotten from his line work at the Edison Company. They prevented my youthful hands from freezing and breaking from the cold. I offered to pay for them, but typical to his gentle and thoughtful kindness, he would accept nothing.

Once when I was at Southern Illinois University, I had serious motorcycle problems and I called Bay. To my thankful astonishment, he and our cousin, Butch Walden, drove four hundred miles to my rescue and aid.

Bay is physically gone to the Lord to be with his beloved wife, Priscilla. However, his memory happily lingers in my mind. I can see his countenance and many of my facial gestures were generated by copying his, so he is nearer than my hands and feet and closer than my breathe.

―――――――――

What now follows is Steve's sibling story. (And, yes, he is including this in his own "Personal Life Story," a book he plans to give as a gift to his three adult children.)

Unlike Mark, I come from a very small family. I only had one aunt and uncle. And, growing up, I only had two first cousins. Sadly, one of my cousins battled leukemia when he was not quite 16 (and I was 19). He lost that battle in under two weeks.

It may be because my dad had only one brother (who died of heart disease at age 8) and my mom had only one sister (as well as twin brothers who died shortly after birth), that both of my parents decided to raise a very small family. So, I only have one brother, Dan, who is five years younger than I am.

BUT WHAT A REMARKABLE BROTHER! Dan is now "mostly retired," after devoting his life as a Chief Financial Officer (CFO), raising money for worthy "non-profit organizations" that help the "most marginalized" members of our society—especially homeless families.

However, that's only one reason why I admire and respect my younger sibling.

You see, Dan is a model of FAITH, HOPE, PERSEVERANCE, and POSITIVITY.

Several years ago (so long ago that I can't recall exactly when), Dan noticed that his slacks and jeans no longer fit over his left leg. Surgeons removed a huge mass that was sent in for analysis, but the test results were inconclusive. His life continued as normal.

Then, years later, another mass developed in his leg. This time, it was identified as cancer. They amputated his left leg above the knee and fitted him for a C-leg—a high-tech device that enabled him to walk. But a serious infection followed, and his entire leg was eventually removed at the hip. No more mechanical limb. It would be crutches and a motorized mobility scooter from that day forward.

But did my brother complain? Did he limp around repeating the words, "Oh, woe is me! Why did this awful thing happen to me?" Not a chance! He remained positive and faith-filled. He continued to give of himself to others! That's just Dan!

Sadly, "Cancer" was not quick to "give up." Years down the road, he was diagnosed with kidney cancer. The medical team surgically removed one kidney. They carefully checked surrounding tissues and firmly believed they had gotten it all. Any grumbling from Dan? Don't be silly! Of course not!

Fast forward to 2019. Cancer again. This time it's Renal Cell Carcinoma. And this time, his doctors told him it's fatal, 100% of the time.

Now, I don't know about you. But that kind of news would have been devastating to me. I would have likely given up. But not my brother Dan. I'm not at all sure, but my guess is that he may have even seen the news as a challenge—an opportunity to take God at His Word: "All things are possible."

Dan identified a Phoenix-area clinic that was blind-testing an experimental chemo treatment for exactly this type of cancer. He signed up . . . in faith.

He is still not sure if he is being administered the "real" drug, or a placebo. However, the most recent images clearly indicate that things are improving dramatically and rapidly. It could be the chemo treatments. Or it could be that Dan Gottry is a model of FAITH, HOPE, PERSEVERANCE, and POSITIVITY!

e. **Spouse:** What about your marriage(s)? What have you learned? What is your best advice regarding marriage?

_____

_____

_____

f. **Friends:**

_____

_____

_____

Here is Mark's Story about "friends:"

The greatest friend that God ever gave me is my beloved Crystal. She is my advocate, guidance system, advisor, helper, encourager, and co-creates the most amazing life imaginable with me.

Crystal is an absolute and complete masterpiece. She is unique in every way. Like a thumb print is a one and only. Her body is artistically sublime, rare, and perfectly curved. Her voice is music to my ears. Yet, most importantly, her mind print is stamped perfect and divine by the creator Himself. There is not another like her anywhere in the world. She is one in eight billion. And I cherish her as mine, a creation divine. I thank God himself for creating a masterpiece that only gets more perfect with time. I am delighted to be her husband and wish her the most magnificent life, with ever better days, weeks, months, and years, yet to come.

Crystal is loved completely by me, our five kids and six grandkids. Life's most precious treasure is creating unending memories of joy, love, wisdom, laughter, and tender times to hold forever in photos and mind.

———————————

And here is Steve's Story:

When Steve was 12 years old, he had a TERRIBLE battle with Rheumatic Fever. (The family doctor told his parents that he'd be dead by 25. They told him that bit of news when he turned 40. He is now in his 70s.) A guy named Jack Janzen pedaled his one-speed bike to Steve's house EVERY DAY to visit him. Steve was literally trapped in bed 24/7. Together, the two guys built an illegal radio station—and the FCC drove 135 miles each way to pull their plug. They also built rockets . . . most of which were simply pipe bombs. They are still friends today.

There are "friends" and there are "lifelong friends." Faithful friends can't be replaced! Now, tell your personal story!

_____

_____

_____

_____

g. **Children**: we believe that we should all affirm the fact that parents/adults CAN learn valuable things from their children. Steve's eldest daughter (the Teacher) taught him that you can STAND UP for what you believe, be OSTRACIZED, and still recover by proving your real worth.

_____

_____

_____

h. **Bosses**: we firmly believe that every job we hold in life teaches us SOMETHING.

_____

_____

_____

Here is Mark's Story about "Bosses:"

Over my lifetime, I have had many clients who could be called my "boss." I have given over 7,000 professional talks or have had paid engagements in 78 countries. I am hoping to talk in all 228 countries—when invited and it is safe. With each talk, I had a client/boss who told me what they wanted their audience to hear. I loved hearing their woes and their wows. I did the best I could to uplift, elevate, and cause positive transformation amongst their attendees. They bossed me, so to speak. I listened, learned, and then created talks to take attendees to the next level. Many of the bosses and attendees have stayed in close touch to me throughout the years.

One example came in a call to me yesterday. I have trained Chiropractors on how to build great healing and health practices with high volume—the Master suggested that ". . . the greatest amongst you is servant of all." One of my great doctor friends, who has a superlative practice, just had an aneurism. He is in terrific shape, fit, well nourished, and absolutely loved by his family, patients, and friends. Fortunately, his wife told me he was in the gym, in a class of about twenty people. Four were nurses. They saw what was happening to my friend and immediately did all the perfect medical procedures that literally saved his life.

His wife said, "God wants him around longer. If he had been in the car alone driving home or here at home with me, I couldn't have been fast enough to call 911 and save him simultaneously." She called asking me to be in his prayer circle of earth angels (I immediately agreed, after stopping my tears) and for all my lifetime of advice, which I freely and completely shared. As a result, he is happily and completely recovering.

At best, we are our own boss. We boss our minds, by bossing our thinking and feelings by telling them how and what to think and feel. We determine what goes into our minds, hearts, and souls by choosing what we see, hear, feel, believe, and choose to experience. It is more important what you exclude, than it is what you include. In the original computer language, the cliché was *"garbage in, garbage out."*

You and I may work for another, but unless you're a literal slave, you choose where you work, what you do and what results you create. Obviously, the goal is to outperform yourself totally.

Choose to boss yourself with a guiding philosophy and principles that are high-minded and commandingly interesting to you, the real boss of you. Live in the spirit of excellence. Promise a lot and deliver even more.

As I write this, I have just returned from my second speaking tour in Vietnam. My client was blown away with the content that I delivered about the seven business that anyone could participate in that will do over fifty trillion, spelled with a T, within the next decade. Businesses included turning trash into cash—i.e. garage profitably recycled ninety-percent back into its original molecules and atoms—so that plastic becomes plastic, glass becomes reusable glass, and petrochemicals become again fuel like diesel, kerosene, and gasoline, plus the other six disruptive businesses. Really recycling garbage and landfills will give us all the clean air, water, and resources that we need for our eight plus billion Earth inhabitants. It is the only way to truly stop global climate change and stop poisoning all of our ground water. The audience loved hearing the solution, instead of just the problem.

I gave every attendee my power points and links to the podcasts, where they could quickly and easily study, learn more, and participate in these omni-profitable endeavors that are destined to positively change the world. I promised and delivered a great and inspiring talk, but the add-ins were enormously well received and eagerly put to use.

Steve's college-era boss, Tom Cousins, at WCCO-TV (award-winning CBS affiliate in Minneapolis/St. Paul, MN) taught him that "A good boss never assigns a task to an employee that he/she isn't willing to perform himself/herself." (He actually lived by that creed, and so did Steve when he owned and operated an advertising agency in Bloomington, MN.)

Now, tell your story about a special boss.

_____

_____

_____

_____

i. **"Encourager:"** Everyone needs one . . . especially ADHD people. An encourager is someone who believes in you and will never give up on you. Mark's encourager was John Reinhardt, whose story you've already read. For Steve, that was the aforementioned Ole Loing.

_____

_____

_____

j. Learn how to "Pay Back" for kindnesses.

_____

_____

_____

As you can tell by the following story, Mark is a true believer in the concept of "paying back."

Everything we have is a gift from God. The air we breathe, the water we drink, the mind with think with, the world we enjoy— absolutely everything. God created it and proudly said: "All that I have is yours . . ." When you contemplate the vastness of the Universe (Einstein said: "Its finite but boundless"), or even the smallness of our Planet Earth with a diameter of eight thousand miles and circumference of 25,000 miles, you have to think, "Wow! And it's all mine to experience."

And enjoy. We are told Genesis 1:26/7 ". . . we are *created* in the image and likeness of God." Therefore, as I understand that, we are here to create and contribute. We are stewards of the Earth, our lives, and our destiny.

Believing all that in my heart and soul, I wrote a book called *The Miracle of Tithing*. Basically, I teach four T's: You are here to give ten percent of your *thinking, time, talent, and treasures* (money or equivalent resources) to charities that you like, trust, believe in, and that are doing great and honest work, with their administrative costs below ten percent. The bonus T is be thankful that you have created surpluses to give. Jesus said in John 10:10: *I have come that you might be abundant.* You and I are not supposed to suffer lack, limitation, or deprivation of any kind. You are here to be abundant. Abundance seems to be underwritten in my experience by contribution.

The oldest spiritual literature on the planet is the Upanishads': the opening line says: *"Out of abundance, He or She took abundance, and only abundance remained."* There is more than enough for everyone, everywhere. And technology creates evermore abundance, jobs, careers, products, services and profitability than ever before in history.

Given my above philosophy, I have tithed to a different charity on every book that I have ever written. I am frequently asked why I have sold more books—according to the *Guinness Book of Records*, over 500,000,000—than anyone else alive. I said, "It is because I am a constant giver."

Currently, my wife Crystal and I are Co-Chairs of the Childhelp campaign to raise one billion dollars to build the Childhelp Global Campus to end child abuse and neglect. (See Childhelp. org.) I can tell you that miracles are spontaneously happening in our lives because we are givers. I recommend you choose in favor of yourself and test the above thinking and see if you don't get an enormous never-ending pay back.

———————

There is nothing all that grand about Steve's Story:

Steve is also a firm believer in tithing, but his story of "Giving Back" follows a different path.

While Steve was in college, as he said, he worked for a television station ... the local CBS affiliate. There, he met a man named Don Stolz, who played animal characters on a daily Children's program. Don also owned the Old Log Theatre, a professional 600-seat venue that offered plays by the likes of Neil Simon (*The Odd Couple* and *Barefoot in the Park*, among others).

Steve mentioned to Don that he loved live plays, and Don said, "Anytime you want to see one of our shows, just tell me and I'll arrange for free tickets." Steve—a student who was struggling financially—jumped at the chance, and for the next two years, saw nearly every play.

He also made a pledge to himself: "When I graduate from college and have a good-paying job, I am going to pay Don back by buying tickets to every show at the Old Log Theatre." And he did. For 33 years. And Don always made sure that Steve and his guests were seated in the front row! They remained friends until Don passed away at age 97 on Valentine's Day, 2015.

2. Major setbacks and what you learned from them:
   a. Wars: Vietnam, Desert Storm?

   _____

   _____

   _____

   b. Financial disasters.

   _____

   _____

   _____

c. Health disasters.

_____

_____

_____

d. Accidents.

_____

_____

_____

e. Relationship messes.

_____

_____

_____

3. Major achievements/accomplishments/victories and defeats.
   a. Awards, recognition.

_____

_____

_____

   b. Education: (Except for Steve's 2 majors, he BARELY made it through the University of Minnesota. Mark has numerous degrees and well as several honorary degrees.)

_____

_____

_____

   c. Unusual/Special achievements.

_____

_____

_____

Mark's personal story:

As world's bestselling author, I have been given many awards. I have gotten numerous keys to cities; ten honorary doctorates from prestigious universities around the world—two in China—and countless charities have asked me to be their spokesperson to help raise money—which I gladly did for everyone from Childhelp, March of Dimes, Boy Scouts of America, Habitat for Humanity, The American Red Cross, and more. I loved doing it. Martin Luther King said, *"Everyone can be great, because they can serve greatly."* I like that thinking, motivation, and admonition.

The single award that I cherish above all others is the "Horatio Alger Award for Distinguished Americans." It means that I have come from rags to riches, been excessively philanthropic, have succeeded in spite of obstacles, and wanted to help 'at-risk kids' get college scholarships, mentor them, and give them a chance at upward mobility, earning power, achievement, and success.

The Association annually bestows the "Horatio Alger Award" on ten outstanding Americans who exemplify dedication, purpose, and perseverance in their personal and professional lives. Recipients have often achieved success in the face of adversity. Each award recipient becomes a lifetime Member of the Association. We have about 250 living members from every walk of life—from astronauts to artists, business people to presidents of Universities. We come together for four days annually and raise phenomenal amounts of scholarship money. The scholarship recipients attend, and we provide them clothes, food, and one of us becomes their mentor for life. It is heart touching and soul penetrating to witness our new recipients get the award from the likes of Clarence Thomas, United States Supreme Court justice. This is the Washington, D.C. event of all events. Everyone is happy, elated, and cheering on and inspiring the students to their respective destinies. It is beyond exciting and memorable.

As a lifelong student of self-help-action books, audios and videos and a twenty-something member of Dr. Norman Peale's Marble Collegiate Church, author of the bestselling book *The Power of Positive Thinking*, my friend, and the co-founder of the Horatio Alger Awards, I secretly admired and privately dreamed that one day I could be worthy of this prestigious award and join the noble names that have won the award.

Speaking at Dr. Robert Schuller's famed Crystal Cathedral one night, I had in my audience Tom Harken's, a Horatio Award Winner and board of directors member, super star business man, and par excellence public speaker. Unbeknownst to me, he nominated me for the award. One bright morning, before dawn, at six A.M., my private home phone rang—a number I had only given to my family and extraordinarily close personal friends. We basically receive two kinds of calls: breakthroughs and the need for emergency help. The ringing phone was a bit of a shock. On the other end was Tom Harken, Dr. Robert Schuller, and George Argyrous—a major real estate owner in Southern California and our Ambassador to Spain.

In unison they shouted: "Congratulations, Mark! You have won the Horatio Alger Award!" "Wow," and "Double wow!," I exclaimed. I was excited, thankful, exuberant, and I lost my ability to speak. It was and is the highest award honor of my life. I plan to live up to its noble advocacy.

Here is Steve's Brief Story:

Steve started an advertising agency fresh out of the University of Minnesota, with nothing more than $125 in cash, a small drafting board, and a used IBM Executive typewriter. As soon as he was able, he hired an administrative assistant. (Back then, there were called "secretaries.")

His very first client was World Wide Pictures, the film division of the Billy Graham Association. Over time, he added several more clients in motion pictures, book publishing, home building, and commercial real estate. He also expanded his office space over the years, and added several employees—art directors, designers, writers, media buyers, researchers, and video producers. His agency won several local, national and international awards, and Steve was in a position to treat himself to some of the "finer things in life."

Steve then focused on earning his pilot's license and Instrument Rating. Clint Eastwood bought his airplane for him (through a movie for which Steve's agency did the marketing and advertising), but Mr. Eastwood doesn't know that. (In fact, the two have never met.)

As the result of becoming distracted by the "good life," (flying, boating, cars, technology, and travel) it didn't take long for the business to lose lots of money and fail. But rather than declaring bankruptcy (a distinct possibility and appealing alternative), he decided to pay off all his debt over time and write a book about his experiences, in order to provide positive guidance to others. His book, *Common Sense Business,* was published by HarperCollins in 2005, and it was featured in *USA TODAY.*

Since that time, Steve has become a full-time author, co-author, ghostwriter, and screenwriter. One of his screenplays for children has been translated into 161 languages and has been seen around the world.

Although Steve should consider retirement, he is very happy doing what he does.

Now, YOUR story!

_____

_____

_____

_____

4. "What other major issues (health, money, career) have you experienced in your life?"

_____

_____

_____

5. "What have you learned from these experiences?" (We believe that your personal life story can offer HELP and HOPE to every reader.)

_____

_____

_____

6. Go Beyond education, where you've lived, career moves.

_____

_____

_____

Writing the Last Chapter of Your Personal Life Story

No one really enjoys thinking about it, talking about it, or writing about it, but that certainly doesn't mean you should ignore the topic altogether. After all, end-of-life issues are something we all have to face eventually.

Here are some of the basic considerations, included to be helpful to you and your family. By no means is it a complete list.

1. Have you pre-planned your final arrangements with a respected provider? (This can help your family avoid "emotional overspending" at the time of actual need. This also helps ensure that your personal wishes will be observed.

   _____

   _____

   _____

2. Have you written your wishes down?

   _____

   _____

   _____

3. Do you prefer cremation, a ground burial, a mausoleum, or donating your body to science? (The prices generally vary considerably.)

_____

_____

_____

4. Do you want a visitation/reviewal? Do you want a military component?

_____

_____

_____

5. Have you selected an officiant? Pallbearers? Musician(s) and music choices?

_____

_____

_____

6. Do you want pictures displayed or a video presented?

_____

_____

_____

7. Do you want someone to prepare and delivery a eulogy?

_____

_____

_____

8. Do you have a Will? Is it current?

_____

_____

_____

9. Does your Will have Codicils? (Legal additions to a Will in which you may specify certain gifts to your heirs and friends. In Steve's case, among other things, he wants a long-time friend to have his set of leather-bound books by C. S. Lewis, and he has designated certain items for his children and granddaughter.)

_____

_____

_____

10. Do you have Life Insurance? (If so, make a list and include providers, coverage amounts, and beneficiaries.)

_____

_____

_____

11. Do you have any ongoing documents? Contracts? Copyrights? Trademarks? Patents?

_____

_____

_____

12. Where do you keep/protect important documents?

_____

_____

_____

13. Who is the executor of your estate?

_____

_____

_____

14. Is there an attorney involved? Name/number?

_____

_____

_____

15. Have you designated a "Power of Attorney?"

_____

_____

_____

16. Do you have a Living Will?

_____

_____

_____

17. Are you an Organ Donor? (This is something we both personally believe everyone should do. It saves lives!)

_____

_____

_____

18. Where have you placed your important documents? How will you family easily find them?

_____

_____

_____

OTHER WORTHWHILE "LIFE" QUESTIONS

1. Write about the most important/significant people at various stages of your life. Why were they so important to you? What did they teach you?

   _____

   _____

   _____

2. Do you consider yourself to be a "Spiritual/Religious" person? (A person of FAITH?) What does this mean to you? How has it impacted your life?

   _____

   _____

   _____

3. What are your Top Ten principles for living?

   _____

   _____

   _____

MARK'S TEN TOP PRINCIPLES FOR LIVING:

1. I believe each human has the intrinsic talent and ability to live their respective destiny.
2. I believe there is "no free lunch:" we all can earn all we are willing to work for in a free-enterprise American System of unlimited opportunity.
3. I believe each of us needs to put in writing what they want out of life—our goals, hopes, dreams, and desires.

4. I believe we are here to experience and express life, liberty, and freedom.

5. I believe we have to cherish the human temple called our body and exercise it daily, eat nourishing food, think positive thoughts, create great and lasting relationships, and have great goals that contribute mightily to our fellow humans.

6. I believe we can take our personal liabilities and turn them into assets for our ascent in life and living.

7. I believe we must control our thinking and feelings to control our lives, the future—and create our future.

8. I believe we can all live abundant lives and create exciting surpluses.

9. I believe in an all loving God—by whatever name—that wants more for each of us than we want for ourselves.

10. I believe we are here to promise a lot and deliver even more (love, joy, enthusiasm, courage, faith, positivity, help, money, hope, than you think you can.)

Steve's are here in a simple graphic created several years ago.

A WAY OF LIFE...

L Learn Something New Every Day!
Laugh Every Chance You Get!

O Order Your Goals and Priorities!
Offer Help and Encouragement to Others!

V Value Your Relationships!
Value Yourself!

E Enjoy Every Day!
Expect the Best!

4. What financial advice do you have for future generations?

_____

_____

_____

5. What are your hopes and dreams for your Children? Grand-children? And beyond?

_____

_____

_____

6. Do you have a "bucket list?" What's on it? Past? Present? Future? What do you still hope to do/accomplish?

_____

_____

_____

7. Was your career satisfying to you? If you could do/could have done anything else, what would it have been?

_____

_____

_____

8. What thoughts do you have on education . . . past, present, and future?

_____

_____

_____

9. What are the best ways you've found to maintain a positive attitude/outlook on life?

_____

_____

_____

10. If you had the opportunity for one "Do-Over," what would be? How about your second, third, fourth, and fifth do-overs?

_____

_____

_____

11. What would you change (if you could) during these stages of your life?
    a. Early childhood/elementary school;

_____

_____

_____

    b. Junior High School;

_____

_____

_____

    c. High School;

_____

_____

_____

    d. College;

_____

_____

_____

e. Graduate School; (Steve's example: "I wish I had gone for an MBA or an MFA.")

_____

_____

_____

f. Marriage(s) (Warning: use your brain here! Your family will read this!)

_____

_____

_____

g. Retirement Planning; (And your suggestions for future generations.)

_____

_____

_____

12. If you have children (and possibly grandchildren or great-grandchildren) what are the greatest qualities they exhibit? Why are you proud of them?

_____

_____

_____

13. Throughout history, who are the individuals you most admired—and WHY?

_____

_____

_____

14. If you could have met and talked to any person—living or dead—who would that person be?

_____

_____

_____

For Mark, it would be Jesus, Andrew Carnegie, John F. Kennedy, Mother Teresa, Napoleon Hill, Ronald Reagan, Neville Goddard, James Allen, Shakespeare, James Clavell, Apostle Paul, Apostle Mark, Apostle John, Moses, Pharaoh, the Sultan of Turkey, Socrates, Plato, Aristotle, and Alexander the Great.

For Steve, it would be Jesus, Moses, Aristotle, Anne Frank, F. Scott Fitzgerald, Walter Cronkite, John Glenn, and Ronald Reagan. In roughly that order.)

15. If you could change any 1, 2, 3, 4, 5 laws on the books (or any parts of the U.S. Constitution), what would they be?

_____

_____

_____

16. If you could live (or could have) lived your life on any other place on earth, what would that place/country be?

_____

_____

_____

17. What vacation stands out in your memory? What country is the best you have visited? What countries and cities you recommend?

_____

_____

_____

18. What are your favorite forms of entertainment? Do you like plays, concerts, Broadway, Movies, Sports events, TV, strip clubs? (Okay, okay . . . just kidding about the last one!)

_____

_____

_____

19. What do you do on a regular basis to maintain your health? Exercise? Diet? Medications? Doctors? Chiropractors? Massage? Walking?

_____

_____

_____

Appendix and Extra "Assignments."

THE LOVE STORY

If you are married (or were married, happily), or you are in a serious long-term relationship, we have a special assignment for you. Write about that important relationship! Then, share it with your special someone! Here's Mark's account of his "finding" his beloved, Crystal.

Not only is he sharing it in this book, but it is included in ASK!, a book coauthored by Mark and Crystal.

If you were to ask me what the greatest miracle of my life was, I could easily sum it up in one word: Crystal. You see, I am *more* than a happily married man; I am a *joyfully* married man. I realize that not everyone can say that. My wife, Crystal, and I have what I call a "twin flame relationship." Twin flames positively and correctly mirror each other in near-perfect harmony. They experience and express a delightful, divine destiny together. They desire to be, do, and have as much for their partner as for themselves. They think and act alike in many ways, yet are strong where the other is weak.

The twin flame relationship is one in which their individual qualities compliment and complete their circle of love. And just as when two candle flames merge, twin flames understand that by coming together, their joined flame burns brighter and with more intensity than they ever could alone. What we share is truly a miracle that is renewed every morning.

A Very Specific Miracle Prayer

There was a time when I didn't think such a miraculous marriage was possible. I went through a season of grief and mild depression after the painful end of my first marriage. Even with scores of friends around me, it felt frighteningly lonely not to be in a marriage anymore. I realized that being married to a true soul mate had been a top priority my entire life, but my failed marriage had cast a long shadow over my heart.

Through much prayer, I kept coming back to the thought that God had painted on my heart long ago, that my soul mate was still out there somewhere, and that I would find her. I started to dream of the perfect woman and to focus intently on exactly the qualities and outcomes I most desired. I sat down and wrote out a detailed list of 267 qualities and characteristics that I desired in my future soul mate. I prayed over that list endlessly, always asking God to show me if I need to add or remove something from my "dream list." I shared the list with my closest friends and prayer partners but no one else. Finding the lady I was describing seemed to border on the impossible, but I clung to the promise God had imprinted upon me. I knew she was out there and, in His timing, I would find her.

A short time later, I was speaking at an aspiring writer's conference in Los Angeles. From the stage, I clearly saw a radiant spirit of a woman in the middle of the audience. I was so drawn to what I saw. She made a dynamic, lasting, and irresistible first impression. After my talk, as I was greeting what seemed like an endless stream of eager writers in the VIP reception, this beautiful lady once again caught my attention. I had learned her name was Crystal and that she was at the conference alone. I wanted so badly to speak to her, but there was no way to politely cut off the people who had lined up to speak to me. I quietly prayed for a miracle—and God responded! Across the room, much to my delight, I saw another attendee wave her arms and inadvertently knock over a full glass of red wine, dousing Crystal's white slacks. It was a beautiful, miraculous mess!

I dashed to Crystal's side and offered my assistance. Since I had spoken at that particular hotel several times, I knew how to get through the ballroom and into the kitchen. I walked her back there to get some club soda for her to use in cleaning her terribly stained slacks. As we chatted, I asked her if she wanted to continue the conversation over dinner. She agreed, and we began an amazing courtship.

Through much prayer, I kept coming back to the thought that God had painted on my heart long ago, that my soul mate was still out there somewhere, and that I would find her.

At first, I thought this miracle was unfolding only in my life, but I soon discovered our relationship was an answer to prayer in Crystal's life as well, as she also was struggling through a failed marriage and a broken heart. In her own words, this is the miracle she was experiencing:

"After a particularly long day of sorting through details of the finalizing of my divorce, what to do with property, and concerns about the kids, college trips, and the like, I fell into bed exhausted and went into deep sleep. In the wee hours of the morning I awoke from a dream that was so profound and so unlike any I'd ever had that I knew God was trying to communicate with me.

"In my dream, I was walking side by side with Mark in a beautiful mountain retreat. The feeling was that we'd just facilitated a life-changing

conference together, concluding the day with a time of answering questions and reacting to comments from the attendees. As we all walked back to our cabins, which lined both sides of a narrow road under the beautiful starry sky, Mark and I felt a sense of extreme urgency and desire to be together alone. It was a holistic feeling that we needed to merge at the deepest level of body, mind, and spirit. We were both relieved when the last person fell away and we were alone at last under the stars.

"As I looked up into the sky, I saw a beautiful pink star, which started zooming toward us. I said, 'Mark, look!' As the star got closer and closer, it became bigger and bigger until it was right in front of us, touching the ground, bigger than both of us.

"Mark shirked back, startled, so I reached over and grabbed his hand and said, 'Don't be afraid. Just look into the center. It's gathering information about us, determining that we can influence so many people's lives for the better.' And then I woke up.

"The dream and all of the feelings and understandings inside of it profoundly moved me. I kept asking God what it meant about me and this man I'd only had one meal with? The answer was there almost before I asked. It seemed impossible that I could have met the person I was supposed to spend the rest of my life with. I wasn't even planning to officially begin dating yet! Even though I knew I needed to keep the order I had planned with my kids, I had a deep confirmation and knowing as I prayed to God throughout that day, that my life had changed permanently from that meeting, and that something profoundly amazing and special was coming.

"When Mark and I did begin officially dating that fall, even though we both had our old baggage to let go of, again and again God kept confirming to each of us that we had found our soul mate in each other. We committed our lives to each other and got married two and a half years later, after my kids graduated from high school and launched into college. We both agree and affirm every day, that everything about my

being at that event, our meeting, the dream that showed us a piece of our amazing future, and all of the other little things along the way, were nothing short of God's divine love intervening on our behalf, to help us find our true love in life. It was nothing less than a magnificent miracle. The beautiful thing is, we get to live the miracle each and every day!"

During the course of our courtship, I discovered that this amazing woman was handpicked by God to be my soul mate. She not only embodied every quality that my friends and I had prayed for; she was so much more than I ever could have dreamed! Finally, under the majestic red rocks of Sedona, Arizona, we were joyfully married.

I tell you this story because I believe it demonstrates an important point in our miracle discussion. And that is, miracles happen to us every day; however, we often turn a blind eye to the incredible daily miracles that add up to a wonder- fully fulfilling and beautiful life! The vision God put in my heart of my soul mate was a miracle. His comfort, strength, and support during my divorce and recovery was a miracle.

The list of qualities He gave me to pray about was a miracle. The burning hope for true love despite my deep heartache and loneliness was a miracle. Bringing me to speak at that writer's conference in L.A.; shining an unmistakable light on Crystal across a crowded room; even knocking a glass of wine out of someone's hand and onto her slacks . . . Miracles!

Miracles happen to us every day; however, we often turn a blind eye to the incredible daily miracles that add up to a wonderfully fulfilling and beautiful life! The vision God put in my heart of my soul mate was a miracle.

But what would have happened if I had ignored each piece of the puzzle He was putting together? What if I had not viewed these things through the miracle mindset, but instead dismissed them as trivial, coincidental, or random occurrences? I shudder to even consider it. Looking back over the course of my life, I see an endless string of unmistakable miracles leading me right into Crystal's arms. And, praise God, I was able to move from one miracle to the next as God wove this love story together!

One Miracle Inspires Another

Matthew Ferry's life was unbelievably busy between marriage, raising four kids, building a new business—and all the financial worries that come with it. He had no time to do the one thing he loved doing—create music. It had been years since he had made his last album, and although the thought of doing another one was constantly on his mind, fitting it in to his schedule seemed nearly impossible. He recalls:

"Some songs were coming, but I was ready for the next one. *I need a miracle*, I thought to myself. I don't need the seas to part. I need the powerful energy of inspiration. I soon realized the reason I wasn't experiencing a breakthrough or a miracle in this area of my life was because my focus was on myself and my business. I was trying to fill a hole in my soul with success, material possessions, and doing the right thing in other people's eyes. But whatever the gain I was experiencing in that area of my life only exposed how much was missing from my life in other areas. My inner voice was yelling, *Contribute! Make a difference! Take your focus off of your needs and see how you can help other people!* Wow! That's what was missing when it came to expressing myself musically! It's time to take my focus off of myself and see how I can help others."

Miraculously, that was about the time Crystal and I had been dating and preparing to get married. Not realizing it, I guess I told Matthew multiple times the story of how I kept asking Crystal to marry me over and over again because I loved hearing her say "yes."

"Mark was dazzled by the miracle that she said yes. And that was my miracle. *Kabam!* The inspiration hit. What if I take their beautiful and romantic story and create a song for them as a wedding gift? Nothing in it for me. Just the joy of creating something that will memorialize their beautiful story. A torrent of energy surged through me. With the unstoppable energy of a tsunami, the words and melody started flooding into my mind. I quickly connected with my writing partner David Keesee, and my inspiration sparked his creativity. Within forty-eight hours the entire song was done. The seas of life did part. The noise and distraction disappeared. God's force, inspiration, and creativity flowed through, and a wonderful song came into being.

"You never know when a miracle is going to happen. And you never know when the miracle you have been looking for reveals another miracle being sought by another."

By the way, go to **markandcrystalsong.com** *and enjoy having, listening, and sharing Matthew's song for free.*

Keeping Your Eyes Open

I truly believe one of the keys to success in our marriages, careers, relationships, and every other area is disciplining ourselves to look for the miracles in life. I refuse to believe that anything happens to us by chance; therefore, each event or encounter, no matter how seemingly random, must have some meaning. That means we have to be vigilant to watch for the miracles that God brings our way each and every day.

Of course, keeping your eyes open to God's often-subtle interventions takes time. This is a new skill you're learning, and you won't be an expert overnight. In fact, Crystal and I take this so seriously that we dedicate the first hour of our day together in prayer and meditation. Much of that time is spent focusing on our marriage and our shared goals for the rest of our lives. But we also spend that time quietly reflecting on what's going on in our lives, who God has brought into view, what new opportunities seem to be coming to the surface, and so on. Day after day, God opens our eyes to all sorts of new miracles, simply because we have disciplined ourselves to *look*. Most people spend so much time praying for the miracles they *think they want* that they have no clear vision of the miracles God is *already doing* in their lives!

Finding Miracles in Unexpected Places

If learning to look for miracles is a challenge for the average person, learning how to see them from the inside of a prison cell must seem impossible. And yet, that's exactly where Bill Sands discovered the most life-changing miracle of his life. And that miracle came in an unlikely form: his captor.

Growing up, Bill's dad was a well-known judge who was strict on the bench and a tyrant at home. Feeling neglected and seeking attention from his father, Bill did what he thought would get the judge's attention: he broke the law—*repeatedly.* By age nineteen, Bill found himself in San Quentin Prison doing an extremely long and hard sentence. And yet, thirty years later, Bill had become a super successful businessman, famous speaker, best-selling author, pilot, boxer, comedian, and even a diamond miner! He lived an extraordinary life and, when he died, he left a legacy of stories, dreams, and belief that life can always get better.

How did it happen? One day the warden at San Quentin, a man named Clinton Duffy, said, "I care, Bill." That alone was a miracle to this young, hurting, lonely criminal who had sought his father's approval his entire life. But Duffy continued, "Bill, you're better than this. Read this book, *Think and Grow Rich* by Napoleon Hill. Let's get you out of the slammer and making a difference." Those words turned Bill Sands completely around. From that point on, he became the model prisoner, which led to his early release. The principles Bill learned allowed him to take control of his life and future. Bill worked hard, studied, built wealth, and wrote a bestseller entitled *My Shadow Ran Fast*. Seeking to be a miracle to other convicts, Bill developed a powerful mentoring program for use inside prisons, which sought to lead men and women out of these institutions and end the cycle of recidivism.

Mark's List of Desired Partner Qualities: The First 112 of 267

About six months into my wedded bliss, I was cleaning my computer desktop and stumbled upon a document called "Soul Mate Goals." I was tickled because I wanted to see how close I had gotten to the characteristics, virtues, and qualities I had so deeply desired in a soul mate.

As I read through them, I was astounded. I realized God had manifested my dreams and beyond for my perfect life partner. Crystal literally was everything I had hoped for and more. I believe that my dreams and prayers were heard and answered.

Here I share 112 of those original soul mate qualities I wrote down. I only share them with you to inspire you to achieve the same or more. If you're already married, may I recommend that you write down everything imaginable that you want in your ideal relationship and see how close you're coming to being that person you dream of. Perhaps, as both of you write out your own journey to soul matedness, later, you will feel open to sharing, comparing, and growing evermore loving towards one another. Often when people are dissatisfied in marriage it's because they're not clearly communicating their most important needs and truths.

My recommendation is that you generate your own comprehensive list. My list is for inspirational and launching purposes only. Remember, whatever you want, wants you. Most importantly, you have to live up to and exceed personally all that you request of another. When I did my list, I knew with the help of my mastermind partners, that I needed to become more of the things I desired and I set to work on myself to accomplish that.

The question you always need to ask yourself when you address your own wants and needs is: "Who do I have to be to attract this woman/man? DO I and will I demonstrate these attributes myself?"

Mark's desires in his future soul mate (**Bold** indicates my absolute "must haves.")

1. Available
2. **Master kisser/lovingly tactile**
3. **Similar values**
4. Has great personal strength
5. User friendly
6. Elegant
7. **Intelligent**
8. **Conservative personality**
9. Great lover
10. Adventure
11. Lives in So. Cal or willing to move here, or we agree to another place
12. Well-traveled and willing to travel
13. **Totally loves me and demonstrates it**

14. Working on self-mastery and spiritual mastery
15. Likes my business
16. Beautiful and takes care of herself
17. **We become each other's number one priority**
18. Excited and enthusiastic about life and living
19. **Vitally healthy, health oriented**
20. Into personal growth and self-development
21. **Happy**
22. Slender and radiantly fit
23. Has a great personality
24. Superb conversationalist
25. **Wise**
26. Witty
27. Wonderful
28. Imaginative
29. Magnanimous
30. Philanthropic before I showed up
31. Fun to be with
32. A Smile
33. Clean, neat, and smells good naturally
34. Inspires evermore love
35. Cooperative
36. Financially savvy
37. Under-spender—lives below her means
38. Has created some of her own means
39. Knows herself
40. Flexible
41. Social graces and practices
42. Wants us to entertain and be entertaining
43. Playful and adventurous
44. Loves to dance

45. Thinks abundance
46. **Wants to create superior memories**
47. **We can talk forever through the decades**
48. Lives in ideas
49. Wants to make the world work
50. **Is passionately on purpose**
51. Sophisticated
52. We have a profound and growing soulular connection
53. **We are soul mates**
54. Loves to exercise, stretch, and work on her strength, health, flexibility, aerobics, and balance daily
55. Wants to see the world
56. Nurturing spirit
57. Has deep spiritual practices
58. Meditates
59. **Creative**
60. **Non-smoker**
61. **Non-alcoholic**
62. **Non-drug user**
63. Charitable
64. Has great etiquette
65. Is pro-organic foods and healthy eating
66. **My friends love and enjoy her personality and are thrilled to be with her**
67. **Loves my family, kids, and grandkids and our kids get along—if hers exist**
68. Culturally, politically, financially, socially, emotionally, and spiritually aware
69. I can fully feel her love for me
70. **Has her own businesses, products, and services to create**
71. My staff loves, enjoys, respects, admires, and appreciates her

72. My career is second to her
73. She helps me know and expand my love
74. **We share similar tastes in almost everything**
75. Energetic and enthusiastic
76. **Wholesome**
77. Fresh, spring-like
78. Young-minded and thinks forever young
79. Neat, clean
80. Original rich mindset
81. Loves me in all my dimensions
82. Disciplined
83. Not jealous
84. **Monogamous**
85. Enchanting
86. Seeks out the good
87. Compellingly joyful
88. Sacred experiences
89. Bright-eyed
90. Eager to learn forever
91. **Wants to serve**
92. **Positive mental attitude**
93. Socially adept
94. **Extraordinary**
95. Proud to be with me and vice versa
96. Great design sense personally, professionally, for the home's interior, et al
97. **Great dresser**
98. **Beautiful to behold**
99. Lives with ease, grace, and spiritual dignity
100. Adoring
101. We give ourselves totally and completely to each other

102. Works on her own well-being-ness
103. Has mutually agreed upon boundaries
104. Truly becomes my best and closest friend
105. Loyalty
106. Trust
107. Faithfulness
108. Integrity
109. **Honesty**
110. Compassion
111. Passion
112. Willing and eager to "Integrate" our two families into one.

Now you've seen the clear intention I wrote about before I met Crystal. In the secret place within my mind, I knew she had to exist and be alive somewhere or I couldn't have had such a clear, purposeful vision of her. I knew she had to be alive and that with every breath I took, I was getting closer and closer.

—Mark Victor Hansen

————————

Steve's Very Short Love Story

I LOVE Mark's story. Because I have known Mark (even before he met Crystal), I know that every word of his story is true. I also know that his list of desired qualities is genuine, and they are all really met in Crystal.

My personal story is much shorter, and my list of desired qualities was similarly brief . . . and it was all in my mind. No need to write them down at that time. Here they are: (As you can see, the first three are the same as Mark's first three.)

1. Available
2. Master kisser
3. Similar values
4. No "bad" habits
5. Not a drug user (or dealer!)

Now, I realize that this admission on my part may make me sound like "Shallow Hal" (from the movie of the same name), but "Master Kisser" was an incredibly important quality to me.

I met my wife, Karla, in 1980, we started dating in 1981, and we got married in 1984. She moved from California to Minnesota just before we met. We were introduced by a friend of mine who was a co-worker of hers.

Some time after we began dating, I chose "our song" and she agreed. It was "Your Kiss Is On My List" by Hall and Oates!

Get Out There . . . Get Known!

One of the factors that contributed to making this series of books possible is that Mark and Steve are in near-total agreement on a lot of things.

And one of those things that we agree on is that if either one of us is asked to write the foreword for a book, or endorse a book or an author, we are likely to do it. (That does NOT mean that we will flippantly endorse something with which we do not agree . . . something that runs counter to our principles or strongly held beliefs.)

There are two primary reasons why we do this:

1. It enhances our "Name Recognition." That's a career booster! (Obviously, it's more of an issue for Steve than it is for Mark. Mark has little problem with name recognition, given the fact that his name appears on the more than half a billion books that have been sold.)

2. But an even more important reason we write forewords and endorsements is that doing so HELPS deserving authors and worthy books! If an author or her or his work are special, we want you, the reader, to know that!

A TYPICAL EXAMPLE FROM MARK:

Here's an example from Mark. It illustrates how one author appreciated Mark's contribution to his success, and now "pays it foreword":

"The idea that none of us is an island in that we are all interdependent upon one another is a foundation of human existence.

"At a critical point in my life when I found myself at the intersection of my hopes and my dreams, Mark Victor Hansen was there to provide me with the inspiration and boost I needed. Today, as a bestselling author, it is hard for some people to imagine there was a time in my life when I had never read a book, much less written one. As a young man, I was an athlete and never focused on books or any other intellectual pursuits. Only after losing my sight did I discover audiobooks through the National Library for the Blind. Now, thanks to highspeed listening via compressed digital audio, I read an entire book every day.

"I had written seven business/success books before I had the inspiration to write my first novel entitled *The Ultimate Gift*. I could have wallpapered my office with rejection letters from publishers until I found one independent publishing group willing to take a chance on my little story. I needed credibility desperately, so I reached out to what at the time was a distant acquaintance, Mark Victor Hansen, to humbly request his endorsement for my new title. Mark enthusiastically wrote, 'I love this book. I see this book becoming one of the great and inspiring movies of all time. It touches my heart and soul deeply, profoundly, and permanently, and will yours too. Happy reading of *The Ultimate Gift*.'

"Those powerful words from a powerful force in the publishing industry like Mark Victor Hansen created the groundswell that changed my world. That little book and three sequel titles, along with the movie trilogy including *The Ultimate Gift, The Ultimate Life,* and *The Ultimate Legacy* have grossed in excess of $100 million and have impacted people around the world.

"Today, when aspiring authors reach out to me for an endorsement, I respond eagerly and quickly because if I live to 100, it will take all those years to repay the positive influence that Mark Victor Hansen created for me."

STEVE'S EXAMPLES ARE DIFFERENT. . . .

Most of Steve's background in writing and publishing is as a coauthor, ghostwriter, or writing coach/college teacher.

So he has asked for encouragement and endorsements from the special people to whom he has offered his services.

Here are some of the responses he's received:

ENDORSEMENTS OF STEVE GOTTRY
AUTHOR, COAUTHOR, GHOSTWRITER, EDITOR, TEACHER

"Not only is Steve Gottry a coauthor of mine (*The On-Time, On-Target Manager*), but he ghostwrote two more of my books; *The Generosity Factor* coauthored with S. Truett Cathy; and *Zap the Gaps*, coauthored with Dana Robinson and Jim Robinson.

"Steve brings three vital skills to my book projects. He listens carefully to all of the relevant ideas, he interprets them in reader-friendly language, and he packages it all in an engaging story.

"I've been so pleased with Steve's contributions that I've referred several other authors to him, including Michael E. Gerber, of E-Myth fame."

—Dr. Ken Blanchard

(Coauthor of *The One Minute Manager*)

"Steve has been a blessing to me in the book writing process. His knowledge, experience, gentle demeanor, and creative sensibilities are among the attributes I appreciate most. He helped me take a project I've worked on for years and pull it all together in a few months. I'm grateful for his expedience and commitment."

—Shannon Cassidy (Author of *The 5% Principle*)

—⚬⚬⚬—

"Steve Gottry served as an amazing editor and thinking partner. This is our third project together to date—I don't think it will be our last. Thank you, Steve!

—Mark Miller, in *The Secret of Teams* (Berrett-Koehler, 2011)

—⚬⚬⚬—

"To Steve Gottry, who was magnificent in putting all the words together, especially after undergoing an emergency quadruple heart bypass. Steve, it's been a privilege and a blessing to work with you."

—Gerard Long, in *The Breakthrough* (Alpha USA, 2010)

—⚬⚬⚬—

"To my great new friend and workhorse editor, Steven Gottry, where would I be without you?"

—Michael Gerber, in *The E-Myth Enterprise*
(Harper Business, 2009)

—⚬⚬⚬—

"To Steve Gottry, my editor and ally, for doing even more than you promised you would."

—Michael E. Gerber, in *Awakening The Entrepreneur Within*
(HarperCollins, 2008)

—⚬⚬⚬—

"Steve Gottry, a friend and collaborative partner who lends his enthusiasm and creativity to a number of my projects."

—Ken Blanchard, in *Zap the Gaps*
(William Morrow, 2002), Acknowledgements

———

"To Steve Gottry for creating characters and settings that bring our principles to life. This book represents one of the most remarkable examples of synergy in which we have been privileged to participate. From the first "kitchen table meeting" involving Ken, Steve, and the two of us, to the final manuscript, this has been a truly collaborative effort."

—Dana and Jim Robinson,
in *Zap the Gaps* (William Morrow, 2002)

———

"Steve Gottry, a friend and collaborative partner who loves to create character and tell stories, for combining his enthusiasm and writing skills to bring the concepts to life."

—Ken Blanchard, in *The Generosity Factor*
Coauthored with S. Truett Cathy, founder of Chick-fil-A.
(Zondervan, 2002), Acknowledgements

———

"As a first-time author, I am honored to have had Steve Gottry as a writing mentor."

—Chris Camillo, in *Laughing at Wall Street*
(St. Martin's Press, 2011)

———

"Steve Gottry relentlessly pushed me to focus on the purpose of this book as he crafted my ideas into carefully chosen words that express my heart."

—Mike Ingram, in *The Master Plan*
(Dust Jacket Press, 2012), Acknowledgements

—◊—

"With humble gratitude to you for making this book something I can be so proud of. You are great, and I appreciate you hugely."

—Rabbi David Lapin, in *Lead By Greatness* (Avoda Books, 2012)
from the author's inscription in my copy

—◊—

REFERENCES FROM FORMER
GRAND CANYON UNIVERSITY STUDENTS

Steve Gottry reignited my love for writing. My senior year of undergrad, I had an extra elective so I "treated myself" to his course. Every week, I looked forward to our classes.

Mr. Gottry was honest about career writing and its rigors. He challenged us with assignments that allowed us to soar and grounded those with concrete editorial suggestions. I probably worked more on our assignments than was fair to my other classes. However, there was something about his standard that made me dismiss grades and work toward excellence for excellence sake.

For a part of my Public Relations thesis—creating a basis for a non-profit—I wrote a picture book manuscript for its publicity platform. Mr. Gottry raved about that piece and my experience in his class stayed at the front of my mind when researching grad school options.

Now, six years later, I have my M.F.A. in Children's Literature.

Out of all my classes with personable and powerful professors at GCU, I remain in touch with only one professor from one class of my final year. That person is Mr. Gottry.

—Rebekah Manley, GCU Class of 2005

rebekahmanley@yahoo.com

—ᴡ—

During my time as Associate Editor for The Echoes campus newspaper, I got to learn under both a practitioner and teacher in Steve Gottry. It was so refreshing having someone with good teaching skills who not only could teach, and do, but someone who would listen as an advisor. He valued my ideas and input and taught me how to become a better writer and journalist.

Corey Batorski, GCU Alum, 2005

Communications/Journalism

—ᴡ—

It is my firm belief that Steve Gottry's class during my time at Grand Canyon University had the single greatest impact of any class I took in college.

"Writing As A Career" was a class that taught different forms of writing and challenged everyone to master different areas of writing. This class also gave real-life advice for everything from writing styles, to becoming published, to marketing a publication. I took many of these elements into my business, founding a publishing company.

I would recommend Steve Gottry to any university and I feel his teaching style is an excellent fit for a university that prides itself on small, intimate class sizes.

Steve's experience as a published author and accomplished writer makes him an immediate asset to the university. It is classes like his which are the cornerstone of how enrollment counselors like myself recruit students to GCU.

—Jeffrey Abramson, GCU Class of 2006
Traditional Campus Admissions Counselor, GCU

—m—

In my life I've had many teachers in and out of classes. In honor of Thanksgiving I want to say how thankful I am for the ones who encouraged me in their own ways. Anne Floyd, Steve Gottry, Karen Costales, Mr. Keefer, Mr. Valencia, Luanne Adams, and Arlene Schnutenous (sorry if I misspelled your name). You are the educators kids today need! I value every lesson learned from each of you! Thank you.

—Starr LaSky, GCU Class of 2005
(From a post on Facebook)

—m—

ENDORSEMENTS ON LINKEDIN

Steve is a creative genius on the inside and the outside. Steve brings the rich combination of both humor and deep insight to every project he undertakes. If you want him to write a book, he will deliver. If you want him to deliver a presentation or workshop, he will deliver. Last, Steve's career is on an explosive upward launch which requires early booking so it is best to call him early!

—Cristi McMurdie, McMurdie Law
(Family Representation and Estate Planning)

—m—

Steve is an amazing writer. He is knowledgeable, perceptive, and funny. He is goal oriented and drives to success in all his endeavors. He is personable and a pleasure to work with. Steve is someone to watch for on the bestseller list!

—Ellen Swan, Honeywell International
(Manager, Obsolescence)

Steve is one of the most creative people I have ever met. He is kind, generous, and has a big heart. If you have the pleasure of hearing him speak, bring the tissues because you will be laughing so hard you will cry. Steve exudes success and positive thinking, and he helps and teaches everyone he meets. If you have the opportunity to work with Steve, definitely take the time to get to know him. Your life will be better for it!

—Angela Leavitt, Mojo Marketing
(Chief Mojo-Making Officer)

More questions to get your creative juices flowing.

Questions are the gift of a lifetime and a life well lived if you keep answering them. Thus, recording your wisdom, experiences, and memories for all future generational progeny.

- Where did you grow up? What was it like? What was important, memorable, disagreeable or special?
- Did you reside in only one home, condo, apartment, or were you mobile and maybe even homeless for a time? How did you feel about your residence or residences?
- Did you like to keep to yourself?
- Did you have one or more friends?
- What's the craziest thing you did with your friends?
- Were you more of a leader or a follower?
- What activities did you do in the neighborhood? (skip rope, play kick the can, hop scotch, etc.)
- What was your neighborhood like?
- Did your parents produce good children?
- Who did you look up to? And down on?
- What was your childhood's favorite toy? What was special?

- What was your most memorable hobby?
- What were your pets? Did you have a favorite? Did your dog like you more than your brothers/sisters?
- Were you a dreamer? What did you dream about?
- Was there an adult in your childhood that you wanted to be just like? Why? Was it their job, clothes, home, attitude?
- What were you family's finances? How did it impact your home and life?
- Did you earn your own money or an allowance? Starting at what age? What were you allowed to spend it on? Did you save money? Did you have your own piggy bank?
- Were you a saver or spender?
- When you went to your first funeral, what do you remember? How did you feel?
- Did you like team or individual sports? Why? What was your most winning moment in childhood?
- Did you watch TV growing up? What were your favorite programs?
- Did you have a best friend? What did you like most or best about him or her? Why? Their personalities, ideas, thinking, or did you have the same set of friends or different over time?
- How were you and your "bestie" alike and different? What made you a good pair?
- Did you have a steady boy or girl friend in high school or college? Or did you change often?
- What was your favorite childhood imagination game?
- As a kid, what foods were your favorites? What did you object to eating? How did your parents react and respond? What do you eat now? What changed?
- Did your family eat together daily? Were there any rituals? How did holidays like Christmas, Chanukah, and Thanksgiving unfold? And with whom in attendance?

- Do you remember the cost of bread, meat, lettuce, and other foods? Did you go grocery shopping with your Mom or Dad?
- Did you love your home town and always want to stay there or move on to new horizons?
- Did you have any imaginary friends or companions? Describe them?
- What did you want to be when you grew up?
- Did you ever run away? Or want to run away? What stopped you or got you home?
- Did you ever get separated from your parents? Were you scared?
- Were you ever sick as a child? (mumps, measles, scarlet fever, polio)?
- What did your family do on weekends? Vacations?
- What is the most memorable experience of your youth?
- Did you pray as a child? Who taught you? Did Mom or Dad pray ritualistically with you prior to sleep?
- Did your parents believe in God? How did they show it?
- Did you experience a close-knit family? What do you remember?
- Remember your first work or job experience? How much did you earn? Did it positively or negatively influence you work ethic?
- Did you, your parents, or grandparents emigrate? Before, during and after arriving what were your feelings?
- What was the distance you traveled to school? How did you get there?
- Who was your favorite teacher or teachers? Why?
- What were your favorite subjects?
- What was your experience and memories of each of the schools you attended?
- Who were your friends at school? Do you stay in touch? Why or why not?
- Did you have any great and inspiring teachers? Did you stay in touch with them?

- Who was the teacher who instilled in you the true desire to learn, grow, and become all you could be?
- What kind of student were you? What subjects did you ace or fail?
- It's said school teaches a lesson and gives a test, whereas life gives a test and you're to perceive a lesson. What tests have you learned from?
- In school were you ever in trouble and got to go to detention hall?
- Were you a "goody two shoes" or trouble maker?
- What career did your father? mother have? Was their work inspiring to you? Did you ever help?
- What was the effect of your parents work on you?
- Were you a reader? What book or books memorably influenced you?
- Do you remember asking or being asked out on your first date?
- Whom was your first kiss? Where were you? Did you like it?
- Did you ever feel like you didn't belong? What affect did it stimulate in you?
- What's the best thing(s) you ever did for your parent(s)?
- Remember your most embarrassing experience? What was it? Who was there?
- At what age did you leave home?
- How do you define love? Relationship? Soulmate?
- When did you meet your husband/wife? What attracted you to them?
- How did you know they were the one?
- How did you propose? Or how were you proposed to?
- When did you feel the stab of love?
- What was the silliest experience?
- What stimulated your respect, admiration, love and trust of them?

- What were your wedding day experiences?
- What were your feelings then and now?
- Did you ever think you made a mistake? (Careful with this one!) What went wrong?
- Were you nervous or "calm as a cucumber?"
- Remember your honeymoon? Where did you go? What did you do? What was the best memory?
- Where did you live when you returned home?
- Did you share the same thinking on how to spend, circulate, and invest money?
- Do you remember discussing having children? If so, how many?
- When did you buy your first home? What did it cost?
- How did owning it make you feel?
- Do you have extended family get togethers? On your spouse's side? Your side?
- What are your religious experiences? Have they changed over time?
- Are you or anyone in your family rich, famous, inventive, accomplished, or extraordinary?
- Who influenced you most in your personal or extended family tree? Why were they significant?
- What is your super talent(s)? don't be modest. Remember even the smallest.
- Did you family embrace or reject diversity?
- Do you feel the quality of diversity?
- What are your ancestral countries of origin? Have you visited them?
- Describe your each of your parent's impact on you?
- Were you the favorite kid?
- What do you remember about your grandmom and your granddad specifically?

- When did you first help someone in need? What did it mean to you?
- What is your philosophy of life?
- How do you define success? Has your definition changed over time?
- Who influenced you the most in your life at different times?
- What is your destiny?
- What's God's destiny for you?
- Have you had a near death experience? How did it affect you? What is your memory of it and perspective now?
- If you only had six months to live what would you do? Whom would you do it with?
- What is your political thinking and feeling?
- How important is money to you? Can you create more of it if you want to?
- Have you studied and worked to master money?
- What's your favorite sport? Are you a spectator or participant?
- In sports, do you have a best statistical performance?
- When did you first learn about sex? Was it frightening or exciting?
- What world events have influenced you?
- Was how you were disciplined as a child memorable, fair, or effective?
- Have you ever stolen anything? If so what? How did you feel? Did you get caught? Did you pay penance?
- Were you a leader in school in any activity (student politics, drama, STEM)?
- How do you spend your free time? Is your leisure spent reading, resting, listening to music, at the movies, traveling, exercising, biking, hiking, swimming, museums, art galleries?
- Are you into advancing technology? How do you see it changing your life and our world?

- What was you nickname as a child? Did you like or dislike it?
- What was your most memorable New Year's Eve?
- Remember your most favorite movies? Do you remember any key lines? How did the movie affect you?
- What is you most unusual experience?
- What is your unusual dream memory?
- As a new parent, what did you feel? Was your reaction a surprise or delight?
- What profound memories do you have of each of your children?
- What would you change about how you raised your children?
- What memorable things have your children said to you? Hurtful, helpful, inspiring, or depressing?
- How many true friends do you have? Make a list.
- How many acquaintances?
- What makes a true and real friend?
- What was/is your greatest fear?
- What would you do to protect your love ones?
- On a scale of one to ten (ten is high) how brave do you feel?
- Have you ever had to defend yourself—verbally, physically, or psychologically?
- Everyone experiences positive or negative addictions—have you ever had to overcome one or more? What lessons did you learn?
- Where have you travelled? What did you learn, feel, and experience? What countries have you visited? Where do you want to visit? Why? With whom? Or do you want to travel alone?
- If it was to be your last meal, what would you want to eat?
- When you felt financial stress, what did you feel, do? Did you seek out expert or qualified help? With whom? Was it effective? Did you know the right person(s) to call? What did you learn?
- Who is the most famous, important, or influential person you ever met?

- Who are your heroes?
- When did you learn to use a computer? What inspired you to learn?
- Did you ever play a practical joke or tease someone? Or have it done to you? How did each make you feel?
- When were you your angriest?
- Can you remember where you were when we landed on the moon, or when JFK was shot, or Princess Diana was killed or 911? How did you feel?
- What were your greatest adventures?
- If you're a grandparent, how does it differ from parenting?
- What is your best Christmas memory? Why? What did you receive or give?
- What are your favorite songs? Music? Singers? Bands? Concerts? Shows?
- The Bible says: "Without vision we perish." Therefore, with vision we flourish. What vision for yourself do you want to flourish?
- What are your best skills, talents, gifts, and ideas?
- Did your parents nurture and encourage your gifts, talents, and skills?
- What did you want be, do, and have when you "grew-up?"
- Did you learn any musical instruments as a youth?
- What did you thrill to do?
- What do you regret doing?
- Do you like your given name? if you could change it what would you want it to be?
- What were your hopes, dreams, and desires as a child?
- What was your proudest moment?
- Imagination proceeds realization, what are you imagining?
- If you could relive any time in your life what would it be?

- If time travel were possible, to what era/year would you go?
- If you could be an entrepreneur and start a business what would it be?
- Are you as happy as you want to be? If not, how could you be?
- Have you kept a journal? What would inspire you do to do so? (It's been suggested that journal keepers live twice.)
- If you could talk to anyone from any time and place who would it be?
- What do you want people to remember you for at your funeral?
- A thousand years from now what would a reader say of what you are writing?
- What do you want your legacy to be? To be sublimely happy what can you create it to be?
- How would you like to change and improve the world? What will you do about it now?
- If your life were perfect what would it look like? How would you make it happen?
- What does my country (America, Canada, England, Australia, etc.) mean to me? What do I want it to be?
- What kind of country and world do I want my children and grandchildren to live in?
- Why do you want to become a millionaire ?
- What do you want to become?
- Will you join the Giver's Pledge of Warren Buffett and Bill Gates?

Additional Resources

Depending on your writing focus (fiction, nonfiction, short stories, screenplays), you will find certain books on this list to be helpful, if not essential. While you may find most of these books in a public library, we strongly recommend that you own these titles followed by an asterisk (*).

THE ENGLISH LANGUAGE

*The Merriam-Webster Dictionary** (Merriam-Webster). Use the thickest one available. The standard for most uses is *Merriam-Webster's Collegiate Dictionary*, eleventh edition. Although you can find access to the dictionary online, it is recommended to have a physical copy of the book, because the definitions will often encompass additional meanings you may not find online.

Roget's Thesaurus, eighth edition. Merriam-Webster also offers a thesaurus. Thesaurus.com is also a resource.

*The Elements of Style**, by William Strunk and E. B. White (Spectrum, 2018). The classic edition of 2018, edited by Richard De A'Morelli, contains the original version, as well as numerous additions.

The Chicago Manual of Style*, seventeenth edition (University of Chicago Press, 2017). An online version of this text is also available through www.chicagomanualofstyle.org/home.html.

The New York Times Manual of Style and Usage, fifth edition (Three Rivers Press, 2015).

Grammatically Correct, by Anne Stilman, second edition (Writer's Digest Books, 2010).

The Associated Press Stylebook 2020 and Briefing on Media Law, revised edition (Basic Books, 2020).

CREATIVITY AND STORY

The Writer's Journey, by Christopher Vogler, third edition (Michael Wiese Productions, 2007).

The Poetics, by Aristotle. Various editions.

The Art of Dramatic Writing, by Lajos Egri (BN Publishing, 2009).

How to Write a Damn Good Novel, by James N. Frey, first edition (St. Martin's Press, 1987).

How to Write a Damn Good Novel II: Advanced Techniques, by James N. Frey, first edition (St. Martin's Press, 1994).

INTERESTING OTHER RESOURCES

Every book of famous quotations you can find. (Internet searches OK.)

Platform: Get Noticed in a Noisy World, by Michael Hyatt, first edition (HarperCollins Leadership, 2012).

A *Dictionary of American Idioms*, by Adam Makkai, M.T. Boatner, and J. E. Gates, fifth edition (Barron's Idioms, 2013).

Dictionary of Theories, by Jennifer Bothamley (Gale Research, 2002).

The Book of Positive Quotations, edited by John Cook, second edition (Fairview Press, 2007).

About the Authors

Mark Victor Hansen

Mark is widely known as an American inspirational and motivational speaker, trainer, author, serial entrepreneur, and member of multiple boards of directors. He is best known as the founder and cocreator (with Jack Canfield) of the Chicken Soup for the Soul book series, with more than 500 million copies sold.

For more than forty-four years, he has focused solely on helping people and organizations reshape their personal vision of what's possible. His powerful messages of possibility, opportunity, and action have helped create startling and powerful change in thousands of organizations and millions of individuals worldwide.

With his open, honest, endearing, and charismatic style, Mark captures his audience's attention as well as their hearts. With his one-of-a-kind technique and masterful storytelling ability, he is one of the most dynamic and compelling speakers of our time.

The Chicken Soup idea was just one of many that have propelled Mark into the worldwide spotlight as a sought-after keynote speaker, best-selling author, futurist, business leader, and marketing maven. *Ask! The Bridge for Your Dreams to Your Destiny* was published in 2020. Mark believes it has lightning in a bottle and it will outsell even the Chicken Soup for the Soul series.

The author of many books such as *One Minute Millionaire*, *Cracking the Millionaire Code*, *Cash in a Flash*, *The Richest Kids in America*, *How to Make the Rest of Your Life the Best of Your Life*, *The Master Motivator*, *The Power of Focus*, *The Aladdin Factor*, *Dare to Win*, *The Miracle of Tithing*, and others. Mark has an extensive library of audio programs, video programs, and enriching articles in the areas of "big thinking," sales performance, marketing, publishing, and personal and professional development.

Mark's energy and exuberance travel still further through mediums such as television (*Oprah*, CNN, and *The Today Show*), print (*Time*, *U.S. News & World Report*, *USA Today*, *The New York Times*, and *Entrepreneur*) and countless radio and newspaper interviews as he assures everyone of the inherent genius in all of us if we choose to access our centers of influence, leverage our strengths, and take action.

Mark is the founder of MEGA Book Marketing University, MEGA Speaking Empire, and MEGA Marketing Magic. Each of these annual conferences speaks to the specific needs of those who want to discover, create, and launch business empires. Mark is now doing these as online classes, please visit markvictorhansen.com.

A passionate philanthropist and humanitarian, Mark teaches the principles of the four types of tithing: thinking, time, talent, and treasures. Favored charities are Horatio Alger Scholarships, Habitat for Humanity, American Red Cross, Operation Smile, OCEANA, the Wyland Foundation, March of Dimes, and Covenant House. He is currently cochairman (with his beloved wife, Crystal) of Childhelp Global Fundraising Campaign.

In 2000, The Horatio Alger Association of Distinguished Americans honored Mark with the prestigious Horatio Alger Award. Each year, this association honors American leaders who personify the virtues and principles inherent in the success stories written by nineteenth-century American author Horatio Alger Jr.

As an award winner, Mark Victor Hansen's extraordinary life achievements stand as a powerful example that the free enterprise system still offers opportunity to all.

In 2004, Mark was inducted into the Sales & Marketing Executive International's Hall of Fame, receiving the Ambassador of Free Enterprise award. He is also the recipient of the 2004 Visionary Philanthropist for Youth Award by Covenant House of California.

In 2000, Northwood University honored him as the Outstanding Business Leader of the Year. In 2002, the University of Toledo presented Mark with an honorary PhD in business administration and established the Mark Victor Hansen Entrepreneurial Excellence Fund, which will help shape the minds of future business leaders and assist in the development of the faculty who will teach them. Additionally, Mark has ten honorary doctorates.

Mark presents fifty seminars each year and serves as chairman of Mark Victor Hansen & Associates, Inc. He is cofounder and chief visionary officer of Chicken Soup for the Soul Enterprises, Inc. and is the president of One Minute Millionaire, LLC.

Mark is an enthusiastic crusader for what's possible and is driven to make the world a better place. Currently he and his wife are immersed in their new venture, which is designed to bring affordable, renewable energy and innovative devices to the United States—and the world (www.metamorphosisenergy.us). Watch an informative video at: www.naturalpowerconcepts.com. Their massive transformative purpose: *energy and water independence for everyone, everywhere.*

MARK VICTOR HANSEN QUOTES

May these quotes inspire you to be rich on the inside so that you live the life of your dreams.

1. The size of my asking determines the size of my result.
2. Every time you get rejected, say, "Next."
3. When you know clearly what you want, you'll wake up every morning excited about life.
4. Turn your troubles into treasures. Learn from them and grow from them.
5. You control your future, your destiny. What you think about comes about. By recording your dreams and goals on paper, you set in motion the process of becoming the person you most want to be. Put your future in good hands—your own.
6. For the next thirty days, think, talk, act, walk, smell, and feel like a business is booming, and it will.
7. Miracles never cease to amaze me. I expect them, but their consistent arrival is always delightful to experience.
8. Money never starts an idea: it's the idea that starts the money.

Steve Gottry

Steve Gottry is the founder and president of Gottry Communications Group, Inc., a full-service advertising agency, and Corporate Channels, a video production firm. Both were based in Bloomington, Minnesota, a Twin Cities suburb. He formed the company in 1970 and served a variety of organizations  across the nation. Among his clients were HarperSanFrancisco, Career Press, Zondervan Publishing House, Prudential Commercial Real Estate, Warner Bros., United Properties, World Wide Pictures, NewTek, Inc., and Standard Publishing.

His firm was the winner of a number of national awards, including three Silver Microphones for radio and an award for direct mail from the International Advertising Festival of New York.

His agency was named Small Company of the Year by the Bloomington, Minnesota Chamber of Commerce. Steve was subsequently recognized as the Small Business Advocate of the Year by the chamber.

Steve and his wife, Karla, moved their family to Arizona in 1996, to leave the colder climate of Minnesota in order to enjoy 320 days of warm sunshine every year. He teamed up with Ken Blanchard in October 1998, to collaborate on a number of publishing projects and has since developed writing relationships with several other best-selling authors.

In 2004, Steve was named writer-in-residence at Grand Canyon University in Phoenix, where he taught a class called "Writing as a Career." He is a current member and past president of Dobson

Ranch Toastmasters. A man of many interests, he is an instrument-rated pilot, an avid semipro photographer, and a devoted Arizona Diamondbacks and Arizona State University football fan. He loves the outdoors and prefers to write at a remote campsite, near the ocean, in beautiful Sedona, or simply out by the pool.

Steve is the author of *Common Sense Business* (HarperCollins, 2005), coauthor (with Ken Blanchard) of *The On-Time, On-Target Manager* (William Morrow, 2004), and coauthor (with Linda Jensvold Bauer) of *A Kick in the Career* (Priority Multimedia Group 2005). He also authored the original "fill in the blanks" book, *The Screenwriter's Story Planning Guide*, which he and Mark have updated and repackaged as *Speed Write Your First Screenplay*.

For many years, Steve and his team did marketing, theater posters, and broadcast commercials for several major motion pictures, including *The Hiding Place*, *Joni*, Johnny Cash's *The Gospel Road*, *Chariots of Fire*, Clint Eastwood's *Pale Rider*, and *Jesus*.

He has written or cowritten the screenplays for four produced television and video/DVD projects, including the script for *The Story of Jesus for Children* (now in 176 languages and viewed by nearly 1 billion people worldwide) as well as *Jacob's Gift* (based on the best-selling book by Max Lucado) and two episodes of *Wondrous Myths and Legends* (Sony Wonder). He also writes, produces, and directs commercial and industrial video projects, and recently won the Aegis Award of Excellence for a pro bono video he created on behalf of UMOM New Day Centers, a group of homeless shelters in Phoenix.

As a ghostwriter, he collaborated with Dr. Ken Blanchard (and the late S. Truett Cathy, founder of Chick-fil-A) on *The Generosity Factor* (Zondervan 2002), and *Zap the Gaps!* (William Morrow, 2002), among others. He did a major edit of Michael Gerber's bestselling HarperCollins release *Awakening the Entrepreneur Within* and contributed to a significant revision of Gerber's book, *The E-myth Enterprise* (HarperCollins, 2009). He recently ghosted *Life through Rosey-Colored Glasses* for NFL legend Rosey Grier.

Steve's website is www.SteveGottry.com.